Land Lines

The Scottish Literary Tour Company Ltd.

Photographs by Marius Alexander and Paul Basu

Editorial text, arrangement and concept © Scottish Literary Tour Company Ltd., 2001

Original illustrative material and photographs © Marius Alexander and Paul Basu, 2001

Landsat 7 ETM © ESA, 2000. Distributed by Eurimage

Polygon at Edinburgh
An imprint of Edinburgh University Press Ltd.
22 George Square, Edinburgh

Designed by Lucy Richards, Edinburgh

Printed and bound in Great Britain by The Bath Press, Glasgow

A CIP Record for this book is available from the British Library

ISBN 0 7486 6304 5 (hardback)
ISBN 0 7486 6305 3 (paperback)

The right of The Scottish Literary Tour Company Ltd. to be identified as author of this work has been asserted in accordance with the Copyright, Designs and Patents Act 1988

Contents

Foreword   ix

Introduction   1

I   The Natural Landscape
        1   The Cool High Bens   5
        2   People of this Glen   15
        3   The Great Wood of Caledon   23
        4   Water Music   31
        5   The Ultimate Island   41
        6   The Might of the Sea   53

II Landscape and Community
        7   Stone and Spire   65
        8   The Life of the Land   75
        9   The Big House   83
        10   Small Town Blues   91
        11   Shrieking Steam   99
        12   Cityscape   105

III The Other Landscape
        13   Fingalian Places   119
        14   On the Road   127
        15   A Cold Ceilidh   133
        16   In the Heather   141
        17   Between Worlds   147
        18   The Skinklan Stars   157

Bibliography   165

Sources of Quotes   168

The Photographs and the Photographers   176

Index of Places   178

Index of Names   180

Foreword

Attempts to capture the spirit of a place in a definition
are rarely fortunate; it is wiser to point to its literature as the
embodiment of a thousand subtle and vagrant traditions.

John Buchan

I first met Moira Burgess to talk about *Land Lines* in a smoke-filled room in Glasgow – amid the back tables in the Mitchell Library coffee-shop – sometime in 1997. The Scottish Literary Tour Company Ltd. was in its infancy, as was the concept of *Land Lines*. I remember attempting to discuss it with Moira, feeling slightly ill-equipped – mapless, even. It was more of a ramble than a preamble! But we got there eventually, I suspect by way of instinct rather than in the implementation of any elaborate plan.

I perceive *Land Lines* less as a narrative text than as a commentary on an existing 'geo-script'. The land is a script in itself, containing powerful and inspiring lines, from which great writers past and present have nourished themselves before passing it on to us. Some of the better-known examples of this strong association with place include Gibbon and the Mearns, MacCaig and Assynt, Shepherd and Cairngorm. *Land Lines* brilliantly illuminates this special relationship which has existed between landscape and literature for so long – if, that is, you see the landscape as a living entity, the embodiment of our ancestors' hopes and dreams.

The publication of *Land Lines* is groundbreaking, ambitious both in its depth and range. I think that it's important to note, perhaps, that the book represents a pivotal element within the larger concept of 'Land-Lines' underpinning the development work ahead and the prospect of a premier dramatised literary tour of Scotland. *Land Lines,* with its unique perspective, so deftly handled by Moira Burgess, has been written as part of this exploratory work in progress and on the strength of many previous and successful literary tour collaborations.

To examine and dramatise 'the literary life of Scotland' is one thing. To attempt to present this exploration in a cohesive trans-regional context, unashamedly packaged for public and visitor consumption and marketed to an international audience, is another – and one which many would describe as woeful indulgence, never mind wishful thinking! The Scottish Literary Tour Company Ltd., however, is committed to this task and is busy preparing to deliver the first part in a matrix of dramatised literary tours across Scotland. I believe implicitly in a national dramatised tour concept and its potential to address both connectivity and emotional memory themes, which to my mind have never been more relevant than today. The model is a powerful one, with its capacity to transcend a multitude of themes and – who knows – some of the requisite dynamic for abetting, to some extent, cultural reunification in Scotland?

Moira has been unfailing in her affirmation and encouragement for this series of dramatised literary tours which the company has rolled out as pilots over the years, across many of Scotland's regions. For that I am indebted to her. She has consistently delivered that essential ingredient – the script – for which actors up and down the land are eternally grateful, and to which they owe their very survival – and I count myself as one of them!

We have brought many people together on these literary journeys over the years, now, and *Land Lines* is a natural extension to this process. Hopefully it will be a treasured keepsake. I hope also that it might serve to stimulate even more people to explore the literary landscape which belongs to us all. Perhaps it is also a starting-point for a yet longer journey exploring that 'other landscape' of which Neil Gunn wrote. To that place between worlds, as subtly coloured as the ever-changing Highland light, which exists somewhere in our memories and which we glimpse from time to time – and yearn for in our deepest senses – Moira Burgess is a sensitive and unobtrusive guide.

The compilation of *Land Lines* has been a long and fruitful journey in itself and will inform and pave the way for a forthcoming pan-Scotland series of journeys in miniature: self-guided explorations of Scotland's rich literary landscape, with accompanying soundscapes. The *Pocket-Line* series, a new kind of literary guidebook, will in turn help to lay the foundations for the first dramatised literary tour of Scotland, widely available and celebrating Scotland's greatness, while maintaining a literary integrity which never shrinks from the truth. And if the truth is what we really seek, then in *Land Lines* and *Pocket-Lines* we look for it in the landscape. Our landscape. The truth between the lines.

Morris Paton
The Scottish Literary Tour Company Ltd.

Acknowledgements

Thanks are due to Viv Devlin for her inimitable excitement and encouragement of the project, Michel Byrne for Gaelic interpretation, and Lydia Kerr for masterful co-ordination; to Alison Bowden and Ian Davidson at Polygon for their commitment and ceaseless attention to detail; to Duncan Robertson of The Scottish Agricultural College for the satellite imagery; and to Jack Paton (senior) for his proofreading and enduring patience.

Introduction

The landscape of Scotland is a rich and beautiful tapestry of mountains, lochs, glens, islands, moors. From an eye in the sky, by aerial or satellite photography, an observer can see the contours and colours, the infinitely complex shape of the land. This eye traces, too, how the landscape has been used and altered over the years: the thick fleece of forestry plantations, the clean lines of farming, the different beauty of towns and cities with their spires and blocks and strings of lights.

But there are details in the landscape which the overhead observer can't see. You have to be there on the ground to appreciate the lichen on a rockface or the wave-scrawled ripples on sand. Then how to convey what you've seen, the panoramic view and the point of perfection? It can be done in photographs, and it can be done in words.

Land Lines looks at the landscape of Scotland through the eyes of Scottish writers. 'It requires great love of it deeply to read,' wrote the poet Hugh MacDiarmid, 'the configuration of a land.' Writers, loving Scotland, can read it, and can take both views, wide and intimate, whether it's Norman MacCaig seeing a 'frieze of mountains' on the Assynt skyline or Helen B. Cruickshank looking at a bird flying across a peaty river pool.

And writers can go farther, doing something which no camera can do. They can tune in to what's behind the landscape. The spirit of place is everywhere in Scotland. The viewpoint near Bemersyde in the Borders known as Scott's View, for instance, is a truly haunted place. It's a fine view in any case, over the fields and woods and the winding River Tweed to the strange, unexpected Eildon Hills, but there's an extra dimension if you know two things. Just here Sir Walter Scott, out riding, was accustomed to stop and look at his favourite view; and, after his death, as his funeral procession passed this way, his own horse, drawing the hearse, paused for some minutes – out of habit? out of respect for its master? – at the accustomed spot.

This interaction between landscape and writers – sometimes called 'literary topography', sometimes packaged in a phrase like 'the Burns Country' – is what we are presenting here. This is not a history or a survey of Scottish literature, so there are famous names which you won't find (as well as less famous ones which you will). You will find some of the romantic poets of the eighteenth and early nineteenth centuries who were so impressed by the mountains and lochs; the kailyard novelists of the late nineteenth century who clung to rural and village life; the realistic novelists of the twentieth century whose concern was for industrial Scotland; and the current flowering of young poets, novelists and dramatists who look at Scotland with new eyes. When a writer is quoted there is often some indication of where he or she belongs in place and time, but you will find more information about writers and their work at the end of the book.

'The landscape of Scotland' can mean several things, sometimes more than one at the same time. There's the natural landscape, the mountains and lochs, the islands in the encompassing sea. There's the human landscape which has grown up as people learned how to stay alive and how to live together, settling beside rivers, building houses and farms, ploughing the land, mining for coal and gold. Neil Gunn entitled his last and most metaphysical novel *The Other Landscape*, and writers have recognised this invisible, spiritual landscape, as well as the natural and human elements, as a source and an enrichment of their work. This book is accordingly structured in three sections: *The Natural Landscape*, *Landscape and Community*, and *The Other Landscape*. Again, readers who want to investigate a particular writer or area will find help in the indexes at the back.

You may be reading this book as part of a Scottish journey or in an armchair at home; discovering memories of past journeys, or planning future explorations. We hope you will finish it with a new appreciation that Scotland is not just a beautiful place, but a landscape of the mind.

I

The Natural Landscape

1 The Cool High Bens

Cauld, cauld is Alnack.
Cauld is the snaw wind and sweet.
The maukin o' Creagan Alnack
Has snaw for meat.

Olive Fraser

It has been said that every Scot is born equipped with a compass in the head. We turn naturally, that is, towards the north, and there are the mountains, 'the mist-covered mountains of home'. They shoulder up across Scotland, great presences, looming ahead however the traveller approaches the Highlands, as the novelist Neil Munro saw. His character in *The New Road* is both charmed and repelled by the Moor of Rannoch, on the borders of Munro's home county of Argyll:

> Eastward . . . the moor stretched flat and naked as a Sound; three days' march from
> end to end they said were on it – all untracked and desert-melancholy . . . The end
> of it was lost in mist from which there jutted, like a skerry of the sea, Schiehallion.
> God-forgotten, man-forsworn, wild Rannoch, with the birds above it screaming,
> was, to Aeneas, the oddest thing, the eeriest in nature, he had ever seen.

The mountains are so old that it's hard for us to grasp their age. We are talking about more than a thousand million years for the grey Lewisian gneiss of the north-west, and 750 million years for the Torridonian sandstone. Continually the land was shifting, folding, eroding; volcanic activity threw up strange rock formations, and glaciers scoured out what are now lochs and glens. We can imagine, if we like, a time when the mountains stood alone, brooding over an empty land. Then the ice released its grip, and there began to be grass and trees, reindeer and red deer, and, some nine thousand years ago, the first human inhabitants of Scotland. All that time the mountains and the rocks were there. The poet G. F. Dutton views an ancient rock, 'clach eanchainn', stranded in the middle of the twentieth century:

> that great stone
> the shape of a brain
> twisted and left there
>
> out on the moor,
> crystals and fire
> fisted within it,
>
> often has seen
> forests go down
> their soil squandered,
>
> seeds blown in
> blown out again,
> ashes and iron

beneath it surrendered.
it was begun
with the first star

is now a stone
sheltering foxes
out on the moor.

often have men
marched through the dawn
to give it a name.

To these first people the mountains were an ever-present fact of life. The process of coming to terms with them, assigning them a place in the human world, began with giving them names. In some cases the names of the Scottish mountains are so old that they have become eroded, like ancient rocks, and the meaning is not clear to us today. We are not certain what our ancestors saw – or what they felt – when they looked at Ben Nevis at the heart of Scotland, greatest of all. Did they see, simply, a mountain covered in cloud? Or a sacred mountain? Or an evil, poisonous mountain? (Gaelic derivations of 'Nevis' have been suggested for all of these and more.) And if we feel an evil presence in the mountains, does it originate from them, or from some element within ourselves?

Other people, in the earliest days, saw other mountains, perhaps, with more down-to-earth eyes. It has been said that Scottish mountain names allow us to see the hills as the first inhabitants saw them: Garbh Bheinn, the rough mountain, Aonach Beag, the small ridge-shaped mountain. Sometimes we may imagine that we hear what they heard: Stob Choire Claurigh could be 'the peak above the noisy corrie', and if the corrie is noisy, it might be with the roar of rutting stags. The modern Gaelic poet Rody Gorman makes stunning use of the names of hills, corries, lochs and mountain passes in his poem 'Leadan'. This is only a part of it:

Bealach a' Chruidh
Bealach an Loin
Bealach an t-Sionnaich
Bealach Coire na Circe
Bealach Eadar dà Bheinn
Bealach a' Ghlinne
Bealach Garbh

Beinn na Creiche
Beinn Dubh a' Bhealaich
Beinn na Caillich
Beinn na Grèine
Beinn an Eòin
Beinn nan Lochan
Beinn an Teallaich . . .

Sgùrr an Easain Dhuibh
Sgùrr an Fheadain
Sgùrr a' Chàise
Sgùrr na h-Iolaire
Sgùrr Sgùmain
Sgùrr nam Fiadh
Sgùrr nan Caorach

Tional nam monaidhean
Gu cruinn na phobal
No mar Ortha nan Gaidheal
A bhios gan seinn
Am fianais Rìgh nam Beann
Mun fhlathas agam fhìn
Gu saoghal nan saoghal
Amen

(Assembly of hills
gathered together like a congregation
or the collection *Carmina Gadelica*
chanted in the presence
of the Most High
in my own Parnassus
life without end
amen.)

As evocative and beautiful are the many colour names. Some are hardly translatable, just as it's hard to put a name to the colour you see on the heathery hill. Cairn Gorm is blue, anyway blue-ish, as mountains seen at a distance are. Beinn Bhreac is speckled like a trout. Braeriach is streakier, like rain-washed scree. Beinn Dearg and Corrieyairack are red; probably it's only a pinkish granite which gives them that name, but the hills in summer always seem to hold the promise of something more spectacular, like the sunset blaze of Ayers Rock. Indeed the novelist Nan Shepherd saw a very similar effect in the Cairngorm range:

> The whole façade is clear, sculptured in block and cleft and cornice, with
> which the light makes play. It is best at morning, when the cliffs are rose-red.
> The phenomenon lasts about an hour, precipice after precipice glowing to rose
> and fading again, though in some conditions of the air the glow lasts longer,
> and I have seen, in intense still summer heat, not only the corries but the
> whole plateau burning with a hot violet incandescence until noon.

It's the air you notice first as you draw breath on the summit of any one of Scotland's hills. Cold sweet air, nothing like the stale chemical-laden stuff in the town. To the poet and novelist Robert Louis Stevenson, remembering the Pentland Hills of his youth, the air – the weather – came first:

> Blows the wind today, and the sun and the rain are flying,
> Blows the wind on the moors today and now . . .

Far away in the South Seas, in voluntary exile for his health's sake, he held to his remembered vision of Scottish landscape. He heard the call of the hill birds, the curlews and plovers – whaups and peewees are the musical Scots names he uses – and he saw the wine-red moor dotted with sheep and standing-stones. What he heard and saw can be heard and seen, magically, through his poem. The sight and sound and scent of the hills comes to you clear and delicious as if you were really standing on a sunny, windy hilltop. And once you have tuned in to that landscape it never leaves you again.

There's something else, though, that Stevenson sees on the hill, or, better, something that he feels. Seeing 'the howes of the silent vanished races' – the green mounds which denote hill-forts and graves from before history – he feels, and we feel, that there's someone on the hill with him, apart from any everyday companion at his elbow. Nearer our own time the Perth poet William Soutar has the same thought:

> Wha gangs wi' us owre the hill
> And is baith far and near?
> Abune the bluid that lifts and fa's
> Anither hert we hear.

There's something behind the landscape. As you travel and admire the scenery and take your holiday videos, there's somebody at your shoulder, unseen.

Who is it? Perhaps it's a Pict. Neil Gunn's character Kenn in the great novel *Highland River* thinks of Stevenson's 'vanished races' as he finds, on his Caithness moor, the prehistoric building locally known as a Picts House. Farther down the strath is a broch which Kenn explored as a boy:

> The stones were so near, the entrance so small. From two thousand years back
> time's fingers could touch them in less than an instant. More than once, indeed,
> Kenn almost felt that touch, jerking his shoulder and body from it and smothering
> it behind him with a cry – a cry, not necessarily, and never quite altogether, of fear.

Perhaps you're in leafy Ayrshire with a line of poetry running through your head, and beside you is none other than Robert Burns, Scotland's most famous poet. 'Ye banks and braes of Bonnie Doon,' he asks, 'how can ye bloom sae fresh and fair?' Because he is sad, he feels, the scenery shouldn't be beautiful nor the birds singing, and his feelings in this place, having found words, somehow remain here.

Perhaps the ghost at your shoulder is closer to home. Perhaps it's yourself as you used to be. The Victorian poet Alexander Smith remarked that you could think of Burns apart from Ayrshire but you could hardly think of Tannahill apart from the Braes of Gleniffer, and, indeed, Robert Tannahill, the gentle weaver who eventually drowned himself because a publisher didn't appreciate his poetry, walked the green Braes above Paisley, in happier days, until the countryside was part of his life:

> Keen blaws the wind o'er the Braes o' Gleniffer,
> The auld castle's turrets are covered wi' snaw;
> How changed from the time when I met wi' my lover
> Amang the broom bushes by Stanely-green shaw!

Or, perhaps, even more difficult to handle, it's yourself as you are now. The hills are eternal, but are you? 'Foo aal's Bennachie?' – how old is Bennachie? – asks Flora Garry, looking at the beautiful Mither Tap which rises above the fertile farming lands of Aberdeenshire:

> Foo aal's Bennachie? As aal's a man?
> Ageless, timeless she, the fickle jaad.
> Lichtsome, hertless she, the bonny quine.
> I've been ower lang awaa. It's me that's an aal man.

It's no wonder that Scottish writers have explored the hills, both in body and in spirit. We know about the Lake Poets like Wordsworth and Coleridge who drew inspiration from the English Lake District (they also visited Scotland, and Keats even climbed Ben Nevis), but the hills are just as closely entwined in Scottish poetry and prose. 'Having been bred amongst mountains,' wrote James Hogg, the Borders genius who turned from farming to writing, 'I am always unhappy when in a flat country'. Hugh MacDiarmid, moving spirit of the Scottish Literary Renaissance in the mid-twentieth century, mused on the view from the summit of Sgurr Alasdair, one of the Cuillin peaks of Skye:

> The Outer Isles look as though
> They were cut out of black paper
> And stuck on a brilliant silver background . . .
> The Cuillin peaks seem miniature
> And nearer than is natural
> And they move like liquid ripples
> In the molten breath
> Of the corries which divide them.

Sorley MacLean (Somerled MacGill-Eain), a bard of the twentieth century whose poetry is as wide-ranging and profound as anything we have from the early Celtic times, has a long unfinished poem 'An Cuilithionn / The Cuillin' which sees the great mountain range of Skye as, among other things, a symbol of human endeavour:

Thar lochan fala clann nan daoine,
thar breòiteachd blàir is strì an aonaich,
thar bochdainn caithimh fiabhrais àmhghair,
thar anacothrom eucoir ainneart ànraidh,
thar truaighe eu-dòchas gamhlas cuilbheart,
thar ciont is truaillidheachd, gu furachair,
gu treunmhor chithear an Cuilithionn
's e 'g èirigh air taobh eile duilghe.

Beyond the lochs of the blood of the children of men,
beyond the frailty of the plain and the labour of the mountain,
beyond poverty, consumption, fever, agony,
beyond hardship, wrong, tyranny, distress,
beyond misery, despair, hatred, treachery,
beyond guilt and defilement; watchful,
heroic, the Cuillin is seen
rising on the other side of sorrow.

MacLean's friend and contemporary Norman MacCaig is in one aspect an elegant and acerbic poet of Edinburgh, but in much of his work he turns to contemplating wild Assynt in the extreme north-west Highlands, its mountains and lochs and glens:

. . . this frieze of mountains filed
in the blue air – Stac Polly,
Cul Beag, Cul Mor, Suilven,
Canisp – a frieze and a litany.
Who owns this landscape?
Has owning anything to do with love?
For it and I have a love-affair, so nearly human
we even have quarrels.

Poets have love-affairs too with individual mountains. Nothing less will quite describe 'Moladh Beinn Dòbhrain/ Praise of Ben Dorain'. It was written – or recited, since the poet never learned to write – in the eighteenth century by Donnchadh Bàn Mac an t-Saoir (Duncan Ban Macintyre, known as 'Fair Duncan of the Songs'), and this translation is by the twentieth-century poet Iain Crichton Smith:

An t-urram thar gach beinn
Aig Beinn Dòbhrain;
De na chunnaic mi fon ghrèin,
'S i bu bhòidhche leam . . .

A' bheinn luiseanach fhailleanach
Mheallanach lìontach,
Gun choimeas dha fallaing
Air thalamh na Crìosdachd:

'S ro-neònach tha mise,
Le bòidhchead a sliosa,
Nach eil còir aic' an ciste
Air tiotal na rìoghachd.

Honour past all bens
to Ben Dorain.
Of all beneath the sun
I adore her . . .

Luxuriant mountain
sprouting and knolled
more healthy and cloudless
than all hills in the world.

How long my obsession!
My song and my passion!
She's the first in the nation
for grace and for beauty.

Donnchadh Bàn's poem on Ben Dorain, which rises above Glen Orchy in Argyll, presents the whole world of the mountain: its woods and heather, its corries and crystal burns, and above all the deer which he loved and observed. As a stalker for Lord Breadalbane he also hunted them, and the dogs which ran down the deer are in the poem too. He spent his last years in Edinburgh and is buried in Greyfriars' Kirkyard, where his tombstone is carved with a stag's head and a gun. On his final visit home he composed his 'Last Farewell to the Bens', recalling at the age of nearly eighty the scenes of his energetic youth. Tradition says he was overcome with emotion and could not complete the poem.

It was late in life, too, that Helen B. Cruickshank considered Schiehallion, the Perthshire mountain whose name, as beautiful as its shape, is thought to mean 'fairy hill of the Caledonians'. Long ago she had heard of a girl killed by lightning high up on the hill, and even then, writes the poet, it was a death she envied. Now, too old to climb, wearied by the threat of pollution and other world problems, she thinks of the hills again:

> And I long to reach the crest
> Of my earthly life, and gain
> Schiehallion.

In this way writers may look at mountains and find they are really looking at themselves. Norman MacCaig, also contemplating Schiehallion, goes farther:

> . . . This means, of course, Schiehallion in my mind
> Is more than mountain. In it he leaves behind
> A meaning, an idea, like a hind
> Couched in a corrie.
>
> So then I'll woo the mountain till I know
> The meaning of the meaning, no less. Oh,
> There's a Schiehallion anywhere you go.
> The thing is, climb it.

Nan Shepherd in the Cairngorms goes deep into the being of the mountain itself:

> So there I lie on the plateau, under me the central core of fire from which
> was thrust this grumbling grinding mass of plutonic rock, over me blue air,
> and between the fire of the rock and the fire of the sun, scree, soil and water,
> moss, grass, flower and tree, insect, bird and beast, wind, rain and snow –
> the total mountain. Slowly I have found my way in. If I had other senses,
> there are other things I should know.

There's one more thing about mountains, if your path takes you to the summit on a clear day. Below you stretches a quilted land washed in the subtle Gaelic colours so difficult to pin down. Here and there is a distinctive mountain shape, a landmark to you and to generations before you. Between the mountains are hidden lochs and beyond them a glint of sea. Looking far, as you would from an aeroplane, from a satellite, from another planet, you see Scotland as never before.

2 People of this Glen

Bhiodh òigridh ghreannmhor ri ceòl is dannsa,
Ach dh'fhalbh an t'-àm sin 's tha 'n gleann fo bhròn;
Bha 'n tobht aig Anndra 's e làn de fheanntaig,
Toirt 'na mo chuimhne nuair bha mi òg.

There'd be young folk singing and dancing,
but that time's past and the glen's in gloom;
Andrew's croft, overgrown with nettles,
reminding me of when I was young.

Màiri Mhór nan Oran (translated Meg Bateman)

Mary Macpherson, the nineteenth-century poet known as Màiri Mhòr nan Oran – Big Mary of the Songs – is looking back, in 'Nuair bha mi òg/When I was young', at her youth on the Isle of Skye. In later life she experienced much hardship for a time and took part in the struggle of the island crofters against their landlords, so that in contrast, perhaps, her girlhood was bound to seem idyllic. However, her image of the deserted croft among the nettles is a powerful one, used by many poets of the Highlands. The underlying theme is not nettles or ruined cottages, but the glen as it used to be.

While the bens, the great mountains, were aloof influences in the lives of Scotland's first people – drawing down clouds, harbouring the deer – these lives were carried on from day to day in the straths and the glens. (A strath is generally a flat river valley, while a glen may be a more dramatic cleft in the mountains.) Songwriters may dwell on the beauty of a glen or a strath – 'yon shady glen' by Loch Lomond, or evening in 'bonnie Strathyre' – but these are, or were, units of population, places with their own life and history, memories and tales. Certainly these tales can be hackneyed at times, as the novelist A. L. Kennedy ironically suggests in her potted history of the fictitious Glen Flaspog:

> . . . the dreadful Massacre of the McIvers, perpetrated by the Evil Red McIver upon his own kinsmen . . . The Evil Red McIver's band of One Hundred Renegades was famed for an unswerving loyalty to its chief. Any member of The Band would willingly jump from the top of the Falls of McIver to his death, at the merest nod of his leader's head . . . None of this is true, of course, but it is far more interesting than a brown and green glen with rocky grey bits and a couple of sheep.

Or there can be a peace so deep, as in Aonghas MacNeacail's 'gleann fadamach/glen remote', that it can be perceived as the peace of sleep, or of something deeper still. Cairns are piles of stones built in memory of the dead:

> plèan a' dol tarsainn
> cho àrd 's nach cluinnear i
> long a' dol sìos an cuan
> ach fada mach air fàire
>
> cuid dhen t-saoghal
> a' siubhal 's a' siubhal

> sa bhaile seo
> chan eileas a' siubhal ach an aon uair
> 's na clachan a rinn ballaichean
> a' dol 'nan càirn
>
> plane crossing
> so high it can't be heard
> ship going down the ocean
> far out on the horizon
>
> a part of the world
> travelling travelling
>
> in this village
> people only travel once
> and the stones that made walls
> become cairns

Yet some of the stories of these glens are both eventful and true. In the far north of Scotland there are at least two beautiful straths, Strath Naver and the Strath of Kildonan, which are steeped in the blackest drama. Their names are lastingly associated with the grim time of the Highland Clearances, a historical episode which echoes again and again in Scottish writing. The novelist Neil Gunn, who was born not far away in Caithness, knew the story well. 'In Kildonan there is today,' he wrote, 'a shadow, a chill, of which any sensitive mind would, I am convinced, be vaguely aware, though possessing no knowledge of the clearances. We are affected strangely by any place from which the tide of life has ebbed.'

It's easy for a traveller to check this out. Just beyond Helmsdale in Sutherland the northbound railway line turns west, because its nineteenth-century builders couldn't get over the steep Ord of Caithness. Rail and road both run alongside the River Helmsdale, and on a fine summer day the strath is an idyllic place, green, peaceful and remote. Wouldn't it be lovely to live here?

Gradually the traveller notices rickles of grey stones scattered over the strath: a broken wall, a gable-end. These are the remains of clachans – farming townships – dating back to medieval times or before. It's possible to walk among the ruins where people once lived and thrived. The historian John Prebble noted how, a century and a half after the glen was cleared, the grass was still greenest where the little potato-patches had been.

The landscape stays in your mind, never to leave it, because this is the Strath of Kildonan, one of the places where tenants were evicted from their homes so that the land could be turned into grazing for sheep,

Fifty years or so after the clearing of Kildonan, the story of the place took a new and slightly bizarre turn, and the traveller can sometimes see stooped figures pottering up and down the Kildonan and Suisgill burns, panning for gold. An old settlement in the strath still bears the name Baile an Òr, the township of gold. But the mini-gold-rush of the late nineteenth century soon fizzled out, and Kildonan is a glen of silence, as Hugh MacDiarmid recognised:

> Where have I heard a silence before
> Like this that only a lone bird's cries
> And the sound of a brawling burn today
> Serve in this wide empty glen but to emphasize?
>
> Every doctor knows it – the stillness of foetal death,
> The indescribable silence over the abdomen then! . . .

When we begin to look for glens with that elusive quality known as atmosphere, then top of the list, probably, is Glencoe in the north of Argyll, veiled in mist and guarded by the mountains known as the Shepherds of Etive, Buachaille Etive Mor and Buachaille Etive Beag. The novelist Naomi Mitchison, always sensitive to the spirit of place, acknowledges their looming threat:

> If you speak ill of the shepherds, speak it low:
> Wait for the winter, they say, wait for the snow,
> Wait for the night of the Campbells, the day of the fox,
> The frayed rope and the boot that slips on the rocks.

Glencoe is certainly a place for poetic mystery. Several of its legends and placenames refer to the Celtic bard Ossian, who is said to have been born beside Loch Triochatan. That sturdy tourist Queen Victoria, for one, wasn't impressed. 'To the right, not far on, is seen Ossian's Cave,' she noted in her journal, 'but it must be more than a thousand feet above the glen, and one cannot imagine how anyone could live there, as they pretend that Ossian did.'

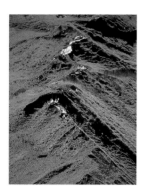

But in slightly more recent times than Ossian's, Glencoe has acquired the name 'the Glen of Weeping'. The weeping arose on a winter night in 1692 when – in the popular version of history – 'the Campbells massacred the MacDonalds,' though it was a little more complicated than that. The trouble began with a decree that the clan chiefs of the Highlands must, by a given date, swear allegiance to King William III. (William was a remote figure in London to the Highlanders of his day, but Queen Victoria was quite worried about her ancestor's involvement in the affair – 'Let me hope that William III knew nothing of it'.)

For various reasons, Maclain, chief of the MacDonalds of Glencoe, was a few days late in taking the oath. Some weeks later a party of soldiers, under the command of Captain Robert Campbell of Glenlyon, appeared in Glencoe and asked for lodgings there, because, they said, the garrison at Inverlochy was overcrowded. They gave their word of honour that they meant no harm, and were made welcome by the people of the glen.

It's thought that Captain Campbell knew all along what was planned, but after two weeks of hospitality he received instructions which left no room for doubt:

> The orders are that none be spared . . . nor the Government troubled with
> prisoners . . . It will be most necessary that you secure the avenues to the south,
> that the old fox nor none of his cubs may get away.

Before dawn on a February morning the soldiers turned on their hosts, murdering 'the old fox', Maclain, and as many of his clan as they could. Though some escaped, all but a handful died in desperate flight over the snow-choked mountain passes. Such a horror – made all the worse by its breach of trust and hospitality – was bound to gather legends as well as truths. It's said, for instance, that the order for the massacre was scribbled on the back of a playing-card, the nine of diamonds, which ever since has been known as the Curse of Scotland. The pipe tune 'Muinntir a' Ghlinne seo' – 'People of this Glen' – was, according to the story, played by a Campbell piper with the intention of warning the MacDonalds to make their escape. Similarly one of the soldiers, sick at heart but bound by his orders to keep the plan secret, is said to have addressed a large stone in the glen in the hearing of his hosts: 'Grey stone, if I were you I would be shifting from here, for great things will happen tonight.'

The very stones of Glencoe, then, are part of its story. Neil Munro plays with this idea in his novel *John Splendid*, making his fugitives see the glen as a nightmare, haunted place, 'forgotten of heaven and unfriendly to man'. But the action of the novel takes place in 1645, long before the massacre of 1692. It isn't a mistake by Munro.

He is raising the often-asked question: is it the stones, the mists and the mountains which supply the atmosphere, or is it the knowledge of the massacre which casts a gloomy veil over Glencoe?

Less famous than Glencoe, yet much loved and written about, are the Glens of Angus – Glenesk, Glen Ogil, Glen Prosen, Glen Clova – which run from the hinterland of douce towns like Forfar and Kirriemuir, in the farmlands of the eastern Highlands, into the deep fastnesses of the Grampians. These are places for walking and fishing, or just for relaxing and breathing the scented air. Robert Louis Stevenson fished in Glen Ogil as a young man, possibly in the Queich burn, though, when he wrote about it many years later, so relaxed had he been that the name of the stream escaped him. He did remember 'a charming stream, clear as crystal, without a trace of peat – a strange thing in Scotland – and alive with trout.'

The poet Helen B. Cruickshank spent holidays in Glenesk as a child during the last quarter of the nineteenth century, fishing, picnicking and searching for blaeberries, cloudberries and white heather. Later in her long life – she was part of the Scottish literary scene between the two World Wars – she returned to the glens to find them sadly depopulated, and evoked the busy scene, now so changed:

> Yet here the clatter
> O' the bairnies' feet
> Aince set the rafters ringin';
> Bess the black collie
> Friskin' at the peat,
> The nearby burnie singin'.

Her best-known poem, 'Up the Noran Water', honours the river of Glen Ogil. It was deep in the glens too, in Caenlochan forest, that she startled a herd of red deer and saw them flee, as a moment of intimacy, she knew, can disappear at a clumsy word:

> Stag, and fawn, and following hind
> Vanished and trackless as the wind;
> Half a hundred wild things gone –
> And dark Caenlochan left alone.

But the Glens of Angus are associated most of all with J. M. Barrie, who was born in Kirriemuir and began his writing career with the 'Thrums' sketches set in this area, collected as *Auld Licht Idylls* and *A Window in Thrums*. Some names and geographical details had to be altered for the purposes of fiction, but 'Glen Quharity' in these books, for instance, can be recognised as Glen Clova.

Barrie later found lasting fame with his play *Peter Pan*, and, though he maintained a connection with Scotland, he was based in London for the rest of his life. It's all the more interesting that he returned to the Glens of Angus for one of his last pieces of writing, 'Farewell Miss Julie Logan', one of the darkest, most haunting stories in Scottish literature. The glen in the story, in fact, is not named, so that as you read you can visualise the glen you know best (as Barrie knew the Glens of Angus). It is remote and narrow, sparsely populated, and for weeks or months at a time during winter it may be 'locked':

> . . . meaning it may be so happit in snow that no one who is in can get out of it,
> and no one who is out can get in. Then, according to the stories that crawl like
> mists among our hills, . . . come forms called the 'Strangers'.

The beautiful Miss Julie Logan may be one of these other-worldly Strangers, or she may be all in the mind of the young minister who is writing his diary. Even years later, long married and settled in a much less spooky part of Scotland, he is still not sure which:

> I have a greater drawing to the foolish youth that once I was than I have
> pretended. When I am gone it may be that he will away back to that glen.

When Neil Gunn made the decision to leave his steady job and become a full-time writer, he began his new life by sailing round the west coast of Scotland in a small boat. Particularly alert, perhaps, because of these circumstances, he came to Loch Etive and found himself haunted by another glen of beauty and legend:

> That evening, as I took the path over the Point, by birch and hazel and oak, with
> Loch Etive down below and more freshness and beauty around than the brain had
> the energy to think on, the refrain of the song *Deirdre's Farewell to Albyn* entered
> and took control.

The story running through his mind is the Celtic tale of Deirdre and Naoise, one of the Three Sorrows of Storytelling. Glen Etive is said to be where these lovers lived for a time in perfect happiness. A wood near Taynuilt is still on the map as Coille Naise, Naoise's wood, and the hill of Stob Grianan on the south bank of the river Etive is said to mark the site of Deirdre's grianan, her sunny bower. Deirdre and Naoise were in flight from the Irish King Conchobar, and it was when they were falsely lured back to Ireland with promises of safety that Deirdre sang her farewell:

> O Glen Etive, O Glen Etive,
> Where I builded my bridal hold,
> Beauteous glen in early morning,
> Flocks of sunbeams crowd thy fold . . .

Rather like Queen Victoria in Glencoe, we may have our doubts about all this. It could be pointed out, for instance, that similar Deirdre and Naoise place-names occur in other areas, notably in Ireland. But Deirdre has a further connection with Scottish writing, because Hugh MacDiarmid claimed her as the personification of Scotland and as the Celtic muse:

> I am with Alba – with Deirdre – now
> As a lover is with his sweetheart . . .

A sunny day among the birch-trees in Glen Etive is a time and place where Deirdre, most beautiful of women, the poetry which she inspires, and Scotland itself, all come to life for us.

3 The Great Wood of Caledon

... Something vast and dark, which clothed the tops
of all but the highest hills, muffled the ridges, choked the glens
and overflowed almost to the edge of the waters – which lay
on the landscape like a shaggy fur cast loosely down.
My mouth shaped the word 'Melanudrigill'.

John Buchan

The Great Wood of Caledon, the primaeval forest, covered most of Scotland for thousands of years from the end of the last Ice Age. In his poem sequence *Sonnets from Scotland*, with its great sweep through the history of the land from geological formation to envisioned future, Edwin Morgan imagines the mystery and the first elusive human inhabitants of the great wood:

Are these bears? Mist. Wolves? Peat. Is there a sun?
Where are the eyes that should peer from those dens?
Marsh-lights, yes, mushroom-banks, leaf-mould, rank ferns,
and up above, a sense of wings, of flight,
of clattering, of calls through fog. Yet men,
going about invisible concerns,
are here . . .

To our Celtic ancestors, trees were important. A verse from *Carmina Gadelica*, the rich collection of folk tradition from the western Highlands, shows us a landscape rustling with leaves:

Tagh seileach nan allt,
Tagh calltainn nan creag,
Tagh fearna nan lòn,
Tagh beithe nan eas.

Tagh uinnseann na dubhair,
Tagh iubhar na leuma,
Tagh leamhan na bruthaich,
Tagh duire na grèine.

Choose the willow of the streams,
Choose the hazel of the rocks,
Choose the alder of the marshes,
Choose the birch of the waterfalls,

Choose the ash of the shade,
Choose the yew of resilience,
Choose the elm of the brae,
Choose the oak of the sun.

They were to be chosen not just for their beauty but for their usefulness. The Great Wood supplied all the timber its inhabitants and neighbours could need for their houses and boats. Ironically, that was one of the factors which signalled its doom.

Climate changes over many centuries inevitably began to bring about the decline of the Great Wood, but the process was speeded up by the activities of man. At a fairly early stage, parts of the densest forest were cut down to remove the hiding-places of wolves and bears, and of human enemies like outlaws and bandits too. Wood was needed for fuel, and later for shipbuilding, at first hand-crafted boats and then on a larger scale. So trees were felled, especially the tall, straight Scots pines.

By the time Doctor Johnson was travelling through the Highlands with his faithful companion James Boswell in the autumn of 1773, the scarcity of trees in the Scottish countryside was something he felt he had to comment on. It might have been just that he was accustomed to the great oaks of rural England, but still he complained: 'The variety of sun and shade is here utterly unknown. There is no tree for either shelter or timber.' Boswell, an admirer of the great Doctor but also proud of Scotland, eagerly pointed out that things weren't so bad in St Andrews, for look! here's a tree!

'Call that a tree?' said the Doctor (or words to that effect). Boswell, abashed, hastened to assure him there was a much better tree a few miles farther on.

Johnson wasn't merely teasing, but noticing social conditions and trends, as he did throughout his tour. The land, he decided, had once been as well forested as anywhere else, but the trees must have been cut down 'without the least thought of future supply.' Farther north, beyond Fort Augustus, the travellers' route turned west, into what was then and still is now the deepest Highlands, and Johnson noted again the effects of felling, this time quite definitely to be seen: 'The country is totally denuded of its wood, but the stumps both of oaks and firs, which are still found, shew that it has been once a forest of large timber'. Whether he fully realised it or not, he was looking at what remained of the Great Wood.

The decimation of the Great Wood, as Johnson surmised, had been going on for a long time and continued for two centuries more. The pine trunks were required for the masts of Viking longships, for iron-smelting, for the ships of Nelson's navy and the Victorian trade boom, for railway sleepers, for the demands of two world wars. Certainly, forestry provided a living for many country communities, and for their lairds, as Elizabeth Grant of Rothiemurchus recognised, writing the memoir of her girlhood spent in the early nineteenth-century Highlands:

Here and there upon some stream a picturesque saw mill was situated, gathering its little hamlet round; for one or two held double saws, necessitating two millers, two assistants, two homes with all their adjuncts, and a larger wood yard to hold first the logs, and then all they were cut up into. The wood manufacture was our staple, on it depended our prosperity. It was at its height during the war, when there was a high duty on foreign timber; while it flourished so did we, and all the many depending on us.

Another money-making scheme of the lairds in that century did, however, damage both trees and dependants almost beyond remedy. The Highland Clearances stocked the hills with sheep and deer, which browsed on the young trees, disrupting their natural pattern of growth.

Scattered fragments of the Great Wood remain. Many of the remaining pines are well off the beaten track, in Glen Affric and such remote corners of the north-west Highlands, but just beyond Tyndrum the railway line to Oban passes a small group of old pines on the hillside. They lift the traveller's heart with their angular beauty, like trees in a Japanese print, because Scots pines are long-limbed and distinctively top-heavy, not at all the shape of the traditional Christmas tree. In Strathspey, travelling by road or rail to the north, it's also easy to see two graceful trees beside the old church in Kingussie – 'headland of the pine trees' – which may have inspired Robert Louis Stevenson. On holiday there for a few weeks, R. L. S. amused himself and his young stepson by compiling a small book of woodcuts and poems:

> The first pine to the second said:
> 'My leaves are black, my branches red;
> I stand upon this moor of mine,
> A hoar, unconquerable pine.'
> The second sniffed and answered: 'Pooh,
> I am as good a pine as you.'

Not far from Kingussie is the Abernethy Forest – the area whose sawmills Elizabeth Grant described – where substantial remnants of the Great Wood have survived. Here the beautiful trees are at last being appreciated and managed so that the forest thrives, and some of its oldest inhabitants thrive too. The wolf and wild boar have gone, but there are pine-martens and red squirrels if you're lucky, along with native birds like the crested tit, the crossbill whose beak is specially adapted to nipping the kernels out of pine-cones, and the seldom-seen capercaillie, the great grouse of the woods.

Sometimes the survival of the Great Wood is signalled by place-names which, as in the case of mountain names, allow us to see what our ancestors saw. Druim a' Ghiùbhsaich, 'the ridge of the pines', above Loch Arkaig, lived up to its name until much of the forest was burned down while Second World War Commandos were in training at nearby Spean Bridge. But the Black Wood of Rannoch in North Argyll, and Glen Derry, 'the wooded glen', in the Cairngorms, not only preserve the memory of the Wood but shelter some of the old trees.

Practical use could be made of the trees, of course, without cutting them down. The resin from which pine trees get their Gaelic name (giuthas, juicy tree) was used for healing ointment and burned as tapers. Rowan jelly is still known as the right accompaniment for venison (though the rowan berries themselves are not palatable to eat) and wine can be made from the birch tree, while willow baskets were for generations part of the stock-in-trade of Scotland's travelling people and gipsies. The rowan and the birch, shorter-lived and lighter-timbered trees than the pine, have not been so devastated by felling. And there's another reason for the survival of the rowan, with its creamy blossom followed by blood-red berries, found everywhere in the Highlands: you should never cut down a rowan tree, because it protects the house, the family and the livestock against evil. 'Rowan tree and red threid,' says the traditional rhyme, 'gar the witches tyne their speed.' Witches can make no headway if there's a rowan tree outside the door.

This is the other element in trees which the Celtic world recognised. They had a mystical importance. The dark yew, being so long-lived, symbolised immortality. That may be why yew trees are often found in churchyards, but it is thought that they may equally have been planted to guard holy places long before Christianity, in the time – if it existed – of the druids. Fortingall in Perthshire is a place full of legend (it is said that the biblical Pontius Pilate was born there during the Roman occupation of Scotland) and its ancient yew may have been a sacred tree. Even more complex are the associations of the little hill of Tomnahurich near Inverness. It is now a cemetery, but is also known as a fairy hill, and its name means 'knoll of the yew trees'.

The birch tree, delicate yet strong, has connotations of beauty and mystery for a Highlander like Sorley MacLean:

> 's tha mo ghaol aig Allt Hallaig
> 'na craoibh bheithe, 's bha i riamh
>
> eadar an t-Inbhir 's Poll a' Bhainne,
> thall 's a bhos mu Bhaile-Chùirn:
> tha i 'na beithe, 'na calltainn,
> 'na caorann dhireach sheang ùir.

and my love is at the Burn of Hallaig,
a birch tree, and she has always been

between Inver and Milk Hollow,
here and there about Baile-chuirn:
she is a birch, a hazel,
a straight, slender young rowan.

At the other end of Scotland the mystery continues in one of the greatest of the Border ballads, 'The Wife of Usher's Well'. The old woman's three sons have been reported dead in a foreign land. In her grief she makes a wish that they may come home. As often happens in ballads, her wish comes terribly true:

It fell about the Martinmas
When nights are lang and mirk,
The carline wife's three sons came hame,
And their hats were o' the birk.
It neither grew in syke nor ditch
Nor yet in ony sheugh;
But at the gates o' Paradise
That birk grew fair eneugh.

That birch tree grows in another world than ours.

But in earthly terms it is a Borders tree, reminding us that the Great Wood extended to southern Scotland as well. The name of Aikwood Tower, which features so strongly in James Hogg's novel *The Three Perils of Man*, informs us that there were oak trees in the area. Mistletoe, which grows on oaks, was the badge of the Hays of Errol. A prophecy by the Borders bard Thomas the Rhymer spelt out the mystic link between the family and the forest:

While the mistletoe bats on Errol's aik
And that aik stands fast
The Hays sall flourish, and their good grey hawk
Sall not flinch before the blast.
But when the root of the aik decays
And the mistletoe dwines on its withered breast
The grass will grow on Errol's hearthstane,
And the corbie roup in the falcon's nest.

And there's Ettrick Forest, though we may wonder about that name, since the green Borders hills are not noticeably forested today. King James V in the sixteenth century brought this about, we are told, with sheep-farming in mind. Two hundred years later, James Hogg, the poet and novelist known as the Ettrick Shepherd, knew all about this. In a letter to his friend Sir Walter Scott he explained: 'The two rivers, Etterick and Yarrow, form properly what is called Etterick Forest, which was the Sylva Caledonia of the ancients'.

And mystery continues in this part of the Caledonian Wood, because, according to legend, Merlin lived here for a time. It's not at all clear whether this was King Arthur's wizard (who in any case can't be securely placed in history) or another bard and seer of the same name, but there's a persistent tradition in Tweeddale of a wild wandering hermit who was killed by shepherds on the orders of a local chieftain, and who is buried under a thorn-tree on the banks of the Powsail Burn.

Loving knowledge of this wood and its legends lies behind John Buchan's novel *Witch Wood*. His fictional village of Woodilee is probably Broughton in upper Tweeddale, where Buchan spent idyllic childhood holidays with his grandparents. The scene is set for us by a present-day narrator looking down from a hilltop on the 'decorous landscape . . . the dapper glass and stone and metal of the village'. But the evening light alters the countryside so that the narrator seems to see 'the Woodilee of three hundred years ago', with the Black Wood, Melanudrigill, pressing close up to its huddled crofts.

The events of *Witch Wood* take place in that seventeenth-century Woodilee. The eager young minister David Sempill, taking up his first charge, knows the place from childhood, but, as in Barrie's 'Farewell Miss Julie Logan', there is something very strange outside his comfortable manse and behind his parishioners' smiles. In parts of the wood, under the birches and rowans, he is as happy as he ought to be. It's when he rides in under the pines that his horse shies and has to be urged on:

> Something cold seemed to have descended on David's spirits . . .
> He recited a psalm, but his voice, for usual notably full and mellow,
> seemd not to carry a yard. It was forced back on him by the trees.

These are Covenanting times, years of religious wars in Scotland, and David meets fugitives, along with a beautiful girl, at the house of Calidon. Can the name, he wonders in passing, be connected to the Latin name for the forest, which, like James Hogg, he knows well? Over and around his story Buchan weaves the mystery of the Great Wood of Caledon, that ancient thing so nearly lost to us, but still, here and there, casting its shadow and its spell.

4 Water Music

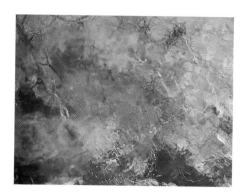

This darksome burn, horseback brown,
His rollrock highroad roaring down,
In coop and in comb the fleece of his foam
Flutes and low to the lake falls home.

Gerard Manley Hopkins

Lochs are the scars left by glaciers moving ponderously, over long ice ages, across the body of Scotland. But when you stand beside a loch that stretches before you into the hills and plunges to an unknown depth, you're looking at something more than geology. The water is dark, or silky blue, or, here and there in the Cairngorms, a brilliant green (these are the lochs where the fairies do their washing). But under the water? What's in there?

The smallest woodland lochan can tease the mind with its mystery. The contemporary poet Liz Lochhead, in 'What the Pool Said, on Midsummer's Day', sees a woman in the pool with her own hidden depths, her fascination and threat:

I've led you on by my garrulous banks, babbling
on and on till – drunk on air
and sure it's only water talking –
you come at last to my silence.
Listen, I'm dark
and still and deep enough.
Even this hottest gonging sun
on this longest day
can't white me out.
What are you waiting for?
I lie here, inviting, winking you in . . .

Lochs have their secrets. On the surface Loch Lomond is a holiday place with its water-sports and picnics. Nothing, surely, could be sweeter and simpler than the traditional song known all over the world. 'O you'll tak the high road and I'll tak the low road,' a lover appears to be singing, 'and I'll be in Scotland afore ye.' But the story is darker than you would think. The singer is a Jacobite prisoner, a follower of Bonnie Prince Charlie, after the failed rising of 1745. He is in an English prison awaiting execution, and the 'low road' is the road by which his ghost will travel to come home after death.

Loch Lomond has the greatest surface area of any Scottish loch and it is also very deep. Rare water-plants are found here, and a fish, the powan (related to the salmon), which is known in only one other location. Because of the depth, the high mountain walls, and the shape of the loch – broad at one end, narrowing to a funnel at the other – sudden storms can whip it to fury, bringing danger to the bright holiday scene. In the interests of safety, tourist brochures have to emphasise not only the beauty but also the treachery. There's more to Loch Lomond than meets the eye.

There's certainly a secret in Loch Ness. Or is there? Coachloads and carloads of tourists pass along its banks, gazing at the polished grey shield of water which (usually) gives no hint of what may lie below. Eyewitness reports of the Loch Ness monster have proliferated since the 1930s, when a new road was built by the lochside, allowing more visitors to the area. Sceptics point at that as the whole explanation. Yet stories of a monster in Loch Ness began long before tourism. In the sixth century, so we are told, St Columba had to dissuade it from eating one of his companions (the sign of the cross did the trick).

And similar stories are attached to other Scottish lochs (not to mention lakes as far apart as Sweden and Canada). Sir Walter Scott reported the long-standing tradition of something in Cauldshiels Loch, near his home at Abbotsford in the Borders, though his keen legal mind deduced that it was probably an otter. In the West Highlands, the monster of Loch Morar (known as Morag) is second in fame only to Nessie, while Loch Awe is the home of Beathach Mor, the Big Beast, which can be heard 'breaking up the ice' in winter when the frozen loch cracks and groans. Then there's Orkney, far to the north, where, well within living memory, strange beasts have been cast ashore dead. Near the beginning of the twentieth century something very much alive was seen at sea, with 'a head like a horse and a slender neck', contemplating a school of whales. The whales had never heard of the Loch Ness Monster, but they were fleeing for their lives.

Loch Ness has been frequently investigated in recent years, and some of the photographs and underwater sonar charts appear to indicate that there's something there. At least in the opinion of believers. Sceptics dismiss them as misreadings of natural or man-made objects (the wake of a boat, a dead horse, two otters at play). Many of them are probably hoaxes; the mood of the tourist, hoping and almost expecting to see something strange, is a favourable climate for both hoaxes and mistakes. The eminent naturalist Sir Peter Scott weighed in on the side of the believers, even assigning the monster a scientific name, *Nessiteras Rhombopteryx* ('Ness monster with the diamond-shaped fin'). It's a pity perhaps that this phrase is an anagram of the words *Monster Hoax by Sir Peter S.*

So Nessie has not in any scientific way been proved to exist. But the eyewitness reports continue, and the belief in Nessie, in Morag and the Big Beast, in the Orkney monsters. Why should that be?

Looking into the dark depths of a loch, it seems, people are bound to give a name to what they see, or think they see. In calm weather that may be a mirror image, another world, like ours but not exactly the same. (It may be worth noting that a calm day is traditionally regarded as 'Nessie weather'.) But that pleasant world is not the whole picture: there are hidden rocks, there is the possibility of a sudden storm. People drown in lochs. It has been suggested that we need a monster in there to make sense of those devastating deaths.

People drown in rivers too. Again there's something in rivers, our ancestors felt, which causes them to drown. Is it the spirit of the river itself? The traditional rhyme about two Borders rivers implies that:

> Says Tweed to Till
> 'What gars ye run so still?'
> Says Till to Tweed:
> 'Though ye run fast indeed
> And I run slaw,
> For ilka man that ye droon
> I droon twa.'

The names of Scottish rivers are often very old. To the early inhabitants of Scotland their river was of the first importance: it could kill them, but it was a source of water, without which they couldn't live. Power of life and death; it's no wonder that rivers were named after goddesses, or, perhaps, goddesses after rivers. Later the god sometimes became a fairy or spirit, like Eiteag who haunts the river Etive in Argyll, or a kelpie, which takes the form of a beautiful horse to lure its riders to a watery death. Later still the Christian church turned these waters of power into holy wells and streams. In his travels among the heathen Picts, St Columba came across a fountain which was worshipped as a god. Anyone who dared to drink from it or wash in it would be struck with blindness or leprosy. It was the work of a moment for Columba to bless it and then demonstrate how he could drink and wash without harm. Many holy wells survive, now associated with the local saint, though there may still be customs – walking round the well nine times sunwise, for instance – which aren't found in any liturgy.

Yet the power of a river is awesome on its own, as Nan Shepherd feels in the high Cairngorms, at the source of the river Dee:

> Here and there in the moss a few white stones have been piled together.
> I go to them, and water is welling up, strong and copious, pure cold water that
> flows away in rivulets and drops over the rock. These are the Wells of Dee.
> This is the river . . . Like all profound mysteries, it is so simple that it frightens me.
> It wells from the rock, and flows away. For unnumbered years it has welled from
> the rock, and flowed away.

Neil Gunn's novel *Highland River* taps into this mystery. His character Kenn lives beside the river (the Dunbeath Water in Caithness, where Gunn grew up) which is part of his life as boy and man. More, it comes to symbolise his life, so that when as an adult he goes on a quest for its source, its discovery is a moment full of meaning. At first he's disappointed, because the water seems to rise straight out of the muddy ground, when he had imagined 'a loch with shores of sand and water grey in the evening light'. But he hasn't quite reached the end of his quest:

> All at once before him again was the tiny stream and lifting his eyes he saw the
> far half of the loch, Loch Braighe na h-Aibhne, the water-head . . . He went on,
> looking at the streamlet, until presently its water grew quiet, seeming to flow
> neither way; and when he came to the loch he saw that its shores were not of
> dove-grey sand but of pure ground quartz, paler than any woman's face in any
> old poet's dream.

And Helen B. Cruickshank comes back after many years to a pool on the North Esk which she knew as a child. This, as it happens, was known as the home of a kelpie, but that's not what Cruickshank is looking for, and not what she finds:

> I mind o' the Ponnage Pule,
> The reid brae risin',
> Morphie Lade,
> An' the saumon that louped the dam,
> A tree i' Martin's Den
> Wi' names carved on it;
> But I ken na wha I am.
>
> Ane o' the names was mine,
> An' still I own it.
> Naething it kens
> O' a' that mak's up me.
> Less I ken o' mysel'
> Than the saumon wherefore
> It rins up Esk frae the sea.

I am the deep o' the pule,
The fish, the fisher,
The river in spate,
The broon o' the far peat-moss,
The shingle bricht wi' the flooer
O' the yallow mim'lus,
The martin fleein' across.

I mind o' the Ponnage Pule
On a shinin' mornin',
The saumon fishers
Nettin' the bonny brutes –
I' the slithery dark o' the boddom
O' Charon's coble
Ae day I'll faddom my doobts.

Another Esk (the name just means 'water'), this time near Langholm in Dumfriesshire, and the other local rivers like Wauchope and Ewes, recur in the poetry of Hugh MacDiarmid, who recalls what he saw in his boyhood there:

Pride of play in a flourish of eddies,
Bravura of blowballs, and silver digressions,
Ringing and glittering she swirls and steadies,
And moulds each ripple with secret suppressions.

And the contemporary poet Rody Gorman celebrates the great river of the Highlands, the powerful Spey:

Nan d' rachadh agam
Air a bhith na mo mhiann rud
Fad ceithir uairean air fhichead,
'S e 'n rud bu rogha leam a bhith
Nam Uisge Spè:

Dh' èirinn air a' mhadainn
Agus, gus do bheothachadh,
Theirginn a-steach dhut nam ghloc-nid . . .

> If I could be anything I wanted
> for 24 hours,
> I'd like to be Spey Water.
>
> I'd get up at the crack of dawn
> and – to liven you up –
> I'd enter you as a morning dram . . .

John Buchan, dreaming of going home to his childhood paradise of the Borders, navigates by the rivers:

> Whaur sall I enter the Promised Land,
> Ower the Sutra or doun the Lyne,
> Up the side o' the water o' Clyde
> Or cross the muirs at the heid o' Tyne,
> Or staucherin' on by Crawfordjohn
> Yont to the glens whaur Tweed rins wee?

And on that route you do come to the great watershed where, in the traditional rhyme, 'Annan, Tweed and Clyde rise out o' ae hillside'. Or near enough, given that the exact source of the Clyde is slightly debatable. The Clydes Burn, the Daer Water and the Potrail Burn all contribute to what will be the Clyde, and soon the growing river has become the spirit of beautiful upper Clydesdale with its green hills and farmlands and blossom-laden orchards. Robert McLellan, who spent holidays with his grandparents there, has left us fine descriptions of 'the garden of Scotland', but he knew that even in this paradise you didn't underestimate the river:

> Mind ye, a man could cross Clyde, if he wasna feart, at a wheen o places . . .
> There was a nerra place atween the banks at the fute o the Linmill parks caaed
> the Lowp, whaur a man could jump across, though naebody had tried for a gey
> while, sin a hauflin frae Nemphlar had landit short, and been cairrit awa to his
> daith. They fand him later on in the pule caaed the Saumon Hole, doun ablow
> the Linn, and he was an ugsome sicht, by aa accoonts.

Farther downstream the Clyde reaches Glasgow. The saying is that 'the Clyde made Glasgow and Glasgow made the Clyde', and the city's river, used and abused through industrial centuries, has caught the imagination of Glasgow writers, like Alexander Smith in the nineteenth century:

And through thy heart, as through a dream,
Flows on that black disdainful stream;
All scornfully it flows,
Between the huddled gloom of masts,
Silent as pines unvexed by blasts –
'Tween lamps in streaming rows.
O wondrous sight! O stream of dread!
O long dark river of the dead!

But on its way through the orchard country, before the industries began to line its banks and blacken its water, something rather unexpected was observed by poets to happen on the Clyde. 'Where down at once the foaming waters pour,' wrote John Wilson in the eighteenth century, 'and tottering rocks repel the deafening roar.' He is describing the Falls of Clyde – Corra Linn, Bonnington Linn, Stonebyres, Dundaff – an extraordinarily beautiful sight in full flow.

From Wilson's time onwards, as poets and artists discovered picturesque scenery, the Falls were on the itinerary of every traveller of taste. Touring Scotland became a fashionable thing to do. William and Dorothy Wordsworth, with their friend Coleridge, left their beloved Lake District to join the pilgrims, and were duly impressed. Dorothy was 'much affected' by the first view of Corra Linn: 'The majesty and strength of the water, for I had never before seen so large a cataract, struck me with astonishment'. Coleridge agreed with the description 'majestic', though not before he had debated with Wordsworth the alternatives 'grand' and 'sublime', because poets have to get it right.

The Falls of Clyde were harnessed in the 1920s for a hydro-electric scheme, and since then they are not often to be seen in full flood. On a few days each year, however, the power-stations are shut down, and the Falls can be seen and heard as Wordsworth experienced them.

Poets are partial to waterfalls. Later in their tour the Wordsworths visited the Falls of Bruar, near Blair Atholl in Perthshire, which they particularly wanted to do, Dorothy wrote, 'for the sake of Burns'. On one of his own Highland tours, some years before, Burns had visited these falls. Unfortunately on that day they were not in full flow. In his poem on the event he gracefully allows his disappointment to be expressed by Bruar Water herself, who 'grat wi' spite and teen,' she admits, to be seen by a bard 'wi' half my channel dry.' If she had been in her usual glory, she points out with becoming modesty, it could all have been so different:

Here, foaming down the skelvy rocks,
In twisting strength I rin,
There, high my boiling torrent smokes,
Wild-roaring o'er a linn:
Enjoying large each spring and well
As Nature gave them me,
I am, altho' I say't mysel,
Worth gaun a mile to see.

So many of Scotland's waterfalls are worth that and more. There's the Falls of Foyers beside Loch Ness, also visited by Burns and other literary tourists, which (before being reduced by hydro-electric works like the Falls of Clyde) got the name Eas na Smuid, waterfall of the smoke, because the mist of its spray could be seen so far away. Norman MacCaig knows the Falls of Measach in Wester Ross:

The wind was basins slopping over.
The river plunged into its ravine
Like coins into a stocking. The day
Was like the buzzard on the pine.

Then there's that great literary waterfall, the Grey Mare's Tail. There are several falls of this name in Scotland, but the graceful cascade near Moffat is the one famously described by Scott:

Where deep deep down and far within
Toils with the rocks the roaring linn;
Then issuing forth one foamy wave
And wheeling round the Giant's Grave
White as the snowy charger's tail
Drives down the pass of Moffatdale.

But there's another quality about a waterfall. Quite apart from the strength of the thundering water, it has another sort of power. Scott doesn't tune in to that, but the twentieth-century writer Sydney Goodsir Smith captures it in his poem 'Omens':

The lane hills and the mune
(Nichtertale in Yarrow
Under the Gray Mear's Tail)
– By me the white coronach
O' rairan linn
Skriddan and cataract
White i the wan
Licht o the sickle mune.

Throw the blae gulph
O' mune and mirk
Athort my vision suddenlie
A lane white bird
– The screich o the linn
At my back, and abune
The far and numenous mune –
Silent, the bird, and was gane.

All the water music is there.

5 The Ultimate Island

Islands are bits of the land
that prefer their own company,
recluses that sea and wind
address in peculiar accents.

Angus Martin

Scotland is surrounded by islands: the holiday islands of Arran and Bute in the Firth of Clyde, the long chain of the Hebrides in the west, Orkney and Shetland in the far north. To those who don't live on one, the idea of an island comes as an image of romance. Islands are misty blue places to dream about, to dream of visiting. If you go there, will you ever be able to leave? Will you want to? The 'Canadian Boat Song' comes inescapably to mind:

> From the lone shieling of the misty island
> Mountains divide us, and the waste of seas –
> Yet still the blood is strong, the heart is Highland,
> And we in dreams behold the Hebrides.

The poem appeared anonymously in the early nineteenth century and its author has never been positively identified (John Galt and Walter Scott are two of the candidates), but that doesn't seem to matter. The exile's yearning seems to strike an almost universal chord.

People brought up on islands, however, can sometimes take a more pragmatic view. You go and come back, by ferry, by plane, perhaps nowadays by inter-island causeway or the Skye Bridge, and you turn a sharp eye on this dreamlike quality. Thus Iain Crichton Smith looks at Lewis from a steamer sailing away:

> Strange to see it – how as we lean over
> this vague rail, the island goes away
> into its loved light grown suddenly foreign . . .
>
> Strange how it's like a dream when two waves past
> and the engine's hum puts villages out of mind
> or shakes them together in a waving fashion . . .
>
> It's the island that goes away, not we who leave it.

The most everyday island can still spark something in a writer's mind. Arran, a couple of hours from the industrial central belt, has long been a Glasgow playground, and its peaks can be seen from unexpected viewpoints all along the south-west coast. 'There's the Sleeping Warrior,' you say with a casual nod. No lone shielings about Arran; it's where you go for the weekend.

Yet poets have been writing about Arran since at least the twelfth century. 'Arran of the many stags,' sang that early bard. Over from the holiday resort of Lamlash stands Holy Isle, so that within a ice-cream's throw of the tourists there's a site which, once a monastery, is now the home of Buddhist monks. In a long poem of our own time Robert McLellan, who lived for many years on Arran, follows the course of an island burn from its source to the sea. As it nears the shore there's noise and merriment, litter and deck-chairs, but he has given us a very different picture of the burn's beginning:

> Look whaur the mist reiks aff the split craigs
> In the hairt o the desolation o creation,
> Whaur the primal convulsions o fire and ice
> And doun the years the weir and teir o the wather
> Wind, rain, frost, thaw and drouth,
> Hae wrocht in the end this unremarkable miracle,
> That beauty is born whaur the corbies craik daith.

Legends cluster round the Arran hills with their Gaelic and Norse names, which, as Robin Fulton sees, make poetry on their own:

> Bharrain, Bhreac, Tarsuinn,
> Nuis, Goat Fell. They made
> huge clouds trickle down quiet glens.

Is it just rain in those clouds? The narrator in one of Naomi Mitchison's short stories is flying back to Kintyre over an island which, though not named as such, is very like Arran. As so often, it is blanketed in white cloud:

> There was a kind of mark in the clouds, a series of dark blotches, very clear in the
> whiteness, coming down the main glen of Eilean-na-caileig where the cloud lay
> piled and still as winter drifts. It was queer altogether, the way these marks seemed
> to be evenly spaced, all pointing in the one direction. Like – like footsteps.

There's more than holiday laughter to be found on Arran.

Legends cling too around the great Isle of Skye. This is the authentic Misty Island, Eilean a' Cheò, and it has been suggested that the name Skye comes from a Norse word for mist or cloud. Alternatively the island may take its name from the Celtic warrior woman Scathach, who taught martial arts to heroes at the site in the

south of Skye still called Dunskaith. Yet another theory is that Skye means 'the winged island', and this is the image used here by the great Gaelic poet Sorley MacLean:

O Eilein mhòir, Eilein mo ghaoil,
is iomadh oidhche dhiubh a shaoil
liom an cuan mòr fhèin bhith luasgan
le do ghaol-sa air a bhuaireadh
is tu 'nad laighe air an fhairge,
eòin mhòir sgiamhaich na h-Albann,
do sgiathan àlainn air an lùbadh
mu Loch Bhràcadail ioma-chùilteach,
do sgiathan bòidheach ri muir sleuchdte
bhon Eist Fhiadhaich gu Aird Shlèite,
do sgiathan aoibhneach air an sgaoileadh
mu Loch Shnigheasort 's mun t-saoghal!

O great island, island of my love,
many a night of them I fancied
the great ocean itself restless
agitated with love of you
as you lay on the sea,
great beautiful bird of Scotland,
your supremely beautiful wings bent
about many-nooked Loch Bracadale,
your beautiful wings prostrate on the sea
from the Wild Stallion to the Aird of Sleat,
your joyous wings spread
about Loch Snizort and the world.

Among the mist-wreathed legends are some which have rather more connection with historical fact, like Bonnie Prince Charlie's voyage to Skye with Flora MacDonald after the defeat of his forces at the battle of Culloden in 1746. Flora's involvement with the Prince was fairly brief in real life, but she has become a heroine of romance, a sort of warrior woman in her own right.

Dr Samuel Johnson and James Boswell, who visited the Highlands less than thirty years after the Year of the Prince, stayed overnight at Kingsburgh House in Skye. Flora and the Prince had lodged there during their adventure, but by this time Flora had married and was the lady of the house. Johnson doesn't go overboard in his journal when describing his hostess: 'A woman of middle stature,' he notes, 'soft features, gentle manners, and elegant presence.' But his emotions were more engaged than he admits, as Boswell's version of the tour makes clear:

> The room where we lay was a celebrated one. Dr Johnson's bed was the very bed in which the grandson of the unfortunate King James the Second lay . . .

Boswell sees this as a rather historic state of affairs (even though, in an early example of political correctness, he doesn't quite like to call Charles either 'the Prince' or 'the Pretender'). It occurs to him next morning that the Doctor and Flora might have cooked it up between them. Flora doesn't disagree, and the Doctor admits that 'he would have given a good deal rather than not have lain in that bed'. The romance of Skye, it seems, had got to the great man in spite of himself.

Skye has that effect on people. Robert Louis Stevenson heard the famous song about Charlie and Flora, which he took to be traditional:

> Speed, bonnie boat, like a bird on the wing,
> Onward, the sailors cry;
> Carry the lad that's born to be king
> Over the sea to Skye.

Stevenson adapted it, turning it into a poem about himself, a meditation on the impermanence of youth:

> Sing me a song of a lad that is gone,
> Say, could that lad be I?
> Merry of soul he sailed on a day
> Over the sea to Skye.
>
> Mull was astern, Rum on the port,
> Eigg on the starboard bow;
> Glory of youth glowed in his soul:
> Where is the glory now?

Skye to poets is an entity, an island with a personality of its own, which affects them even as they think they are observing it.

Far to the north-east, Orkney and Shetland are sometimes described together as 'the Northern Isles', often boxed together in the corner of an atlas page, categorised, in fact, as the same sort of place. Nothing could be more mistaken. Different from the rest of Scotland, they are also completely different from each other. It can be a surprise for the visitor to discover this, but it is something that Orkneymen and Shetlanders, and their poets, have known all along.

The first landmark in Orkney literature is the *Orkneyinga Saga*, the eventful history of the Earls of Orkney, probably written in the early thirteenth century. So much of Orkney's history can still be traced above ground that the saga can be used, in parts, as a guidebook. It's possible to stand at Orphir, for instance, among the remains of the very buildings described: 'There was a great drinking-hall at Orphir . . . and in front of the hall, just a few paces down from it, stood a fine church'. The saga mentions Kolbein Hruga, who built 'a fine stone fort' on the island of Wyre, and its ruins, now known as Cubbie Roo's Castle, can still be seen. One of Kolbein's sons, Bjarni, was a poet. Strangely, centuries later, another Orkney poet spent an idyllic, impressionable childhood on the same tiny island. Edwin Muir moved with his family to a grimmer life in Glasgow and a later career as writer and translator, but Wyre remained with him:

> Over the sound a ship so slow would pass
> That in the black hill's gloom it seemed to lie.
> The evening sound was smooth like sunken glass,
> And time seemed finished ere the ship passed by.

The novelist Eric Linklater – who was not born in Orkney, but maintained that he had been conceived there, and made his home there for many years – puts his finger on the unique element of the Orkney landscape:

> Light is the dominating factor in its scenery . . . Except Hoy, there are no hills
> high enough to intercept it. There are no trees to diminish it. There is, on the
> entire circumference, the sea to reflect it.

And Robert Rendall in a few beautiful poems, often in the soft Orkney dialect, sets island life against a timeless backdrop:

> The winter lift is glintan doun
> Wi' tullimentan stars besprent,
> As were the very heavens abune
> Clean gyte wi' frosty merriment,
> Their lowan e'en are taakan tent
> O' chiels like Mansie o' the Bu
> Whase days upon the land are spent
> Ruggan wi' Taurus and the Pleugh.

But the poet who brings Orkney to life is George Mackay Brown. He was born in Stromness, which he called 'Hamnavoe' in his poetry:

> My father passed with his penny letters
> Through closes opening and shutting like legends
> When barbarous with gulls
> Hamnavoe's morning broke
>
> On the salt and tar steps. Herring boats,
> Puffing red sails, the tillers
> Of cold horizons, leaned
> Down the gull-gaunt tide . . .

Apart from a few years as a student – when Edwin Muir encouraged his writing – George Mackay Brown continued to live in Stromness and set virtually all his work in Orkney, weaving its history, life and landscape into his poetry and fiction. It's still impossible to visit Stromness without thinking of him, seeing 'the twelve piers of Hamnavoe' with his eyes:

> Those huge apostle feet
> Stand in the ebb.
> > Twice daily
> The god of whale and iceberg
> Returns with gulls
> To lay green blessings on them . . .

There's a saying that Orkneymen are crofters with boats, while Shetlanders are fishermen with ploughs. The poet Hugh MacDiarmid spent nine years with his family on the Shetland island of Whalsay, in a cottage which he rented for twenty-seven shillings a year. It was a time of seeking a subsistence living from land and sea, though he said later that he did get a lot of writing done. The cottage, then colourfully known as Sodom (though this is only Sudheim, 'southern home'), is now named Grieve House, and has in recent years been used as a böd, a spartan but evocative type of holiday house.

The rich Shetland dialect has been used to advantage by writers. Robert Alan Jamieson, the young Shetland poet and novelist, called an early collection of poetry *Shoormal*, explaining that 'da shoormal' is 'the shallows on a beach: the space between the tides where the moon weighs the density of the ocean' but here symbolises 'the flow and ebb of the local dialect'. It is in full flow in the poems of 'Vagaland' (the pen-name of T. A. Robertson):

> Oot bewast da Horn o Papa,
>   Rowin Foula doon!
> Ower a hidden piece o water,
>   Rowin Foula doon!
> Roond da boat da tide-lumps makkin
> Sunlicht trowe da cloods is brakkin;
> We maan geng whaar fish is takkin,
>   Rowin Foula doon!

These are 'Papa men', fishermen from the small island of Papa Stour, and they are rowing so far west that the high cliffs of Foula drop under the horizon behind them. If all else failed, it's said, Papa men could navigate their way home by the scent of wildflowers on Papa Stour.

'Vagaland' also celebrated the beauty of the brief summer on the mainland of Shetland: 'a glöd o blue an gold,' he wrote, 'a glisk o white an green.' Writing as he was, however, in the early and mid-twentieth century, he also saw ruined walls and fields taken over by rushes as the crofters left the land to find employment elsewhere:

> You see noo, every saison,
> Run waas o barns an byres,
> An riggs an cuts fast shangin
> Ta burra an ta mires,
> An little reek fae fires . . .

Then came the oil, discovered in the North Sea and brought ashore to great terminals like Sullom Voe in Shetland from the 1970s onwards. Industry, new housing, improved infrastructure and facilities, all came to Shetland at once, greatly changing both landscape and life in the islands. It is probably too soon to say for certain how permanent and how beneficial these changes have been. Robert Alan Jamieson begins the process in his novel *Thin Wealth*:

> In the voar number of the *New Shetlander*, local cartoonist F. S. Walterson depicted
> the traditional 'auld croftin wife' at the side of her peat stack, setting off a maroon,
> while at sea the shape of a tanker courting an oil well completed the composition.
> The sketch was captioned 'Calling him in fae da rig'; a pun centred on the dialect
> word for 'field' which now had another meaning . . .

In the Hebrides, or Western Isles, the culture and literature are Gaelic. The string of islands stretching from the Butt of Lewis in the north to Barra Head in the south is sometimes called the Long Island, but, just as in Orkney and Shetland, this overlooks the differences to be found between one island and the next.

Writers from mainland Scotland, finding contrasts in attitudes, in scenery, in weather, have also tended to find what they want to find, sometimes romance and mystery, sometimes humour (as in Compton Mackenzie's novel *Whisky Galore*, based on the real-life shipwreck on Eriskay of the S. S. *Politician* with a cargo of whisky). But writers brought up in the islands give us a different perspective. Their voices are strongly heard now that the Gaelic language, for long undervalued or even forbidden, is flourishing again. Iain Crichton Smith remembers Lewis as a bare land of moor and sea, which nevertheless he loves. Though it doesn't fit the conventional idea of a poetic place, he finds poetry there:

> But it was the fine bareness of Lewis
> that made the work of my head
> like a loom full of the music
> of the miracles and nobility of our time.

And Derick Thomson, also from Lewis, considers, on a visit home, the relationship between himself and the land and God:

Is gann gu faca mi Hòl am bliadhna,
bha e air fàs cho beag;
feumaidh gu robh 'n Cruthaighear trang
leis an tarbh-chrann,
a' sgrìobadh a' mhullaich dheth
a bha cho àrd 's cho fionnar
's ga charadh aig a' bhonn,
a' toirt air falbh a chaisead,
agus is dòcha a mhaise,
ga lìomhadh gus a robh a chruth
air a chall.

Air a neo
's ann ormsa bha E 'g obair.

'S mas ann
dè eile rinn E orm?

I hardly noticed Hol this year,
it has become so small a hill;
the Creator must have been busy
with the bulldozer
scraping away at its summit
that was so high and so fresh
and depositing it at the foot,
robbing it of its steepness
and perhaps of its beauty,
smoothing it until its lines
were lost.

Alternatively
He was at work on me.

And if so,
what else did He do to me?

Far out in the Atlantic, fifty miles west of the Western Isles, lie the islands that make up St Kilda. The islanders were evacuated at their own request in 1930, when the population had declined to a point where it was impossible to survive. The end came at least partly through the impact of modern civilisation – its news, its ideas, its imported goods – and for that among other reasons a fascination with their way of life persists. Douglas Dunn considers 'St Kilda's Parliament', the daily gathering of St Kilda men which directed the island's life:

> It is a remote democracy, where men,
> In manacles of place, outstare a sea
> That rattles back its manacles of salt,
> The moody jailer of the wild Atlantic.

St Kilda is now occupied again – it belongs to the National Trust for Scotland and has been a nature reserve and a rocket tracking station in the years since the evacuation – but the old life has, of course, gone. Was it worth saving? Was it a paradise, or was it a dead end? (The name St Kilda is probably due to a mapmaker's error, the correct name for the main island of the group being Hirta. It's been suggested that this is connected to an Old Irish word meaning 'death'.)

Is an island paradise to be found anywhere now? From the summit of Cairngorm, one midsummer day, Nan Shepherd looked 'out past Ben Nevis to Morar', and, she thought, 'further even than that'. There were no islands in that direction, she knew, but:

> I could have sworn I saw a shape, distinct and blue, very clear and small, further
> off than any hill the chart recorded. The chart was against me, my companions
> were against me, I never saw it again. On a day like that, height goes to one's head.
> Perhaps it was the lost Atlantis focused for a moment out of time.

Or perhaps, shaded by distance, it was the Green Island, one form of the Celtic otherworld. The legend was well known to Neil Gunn, who used it in his novel *The Green Isle of the Great Deep*, with a difference, for his Green Isle is a totalitarian state. The twist is all the more bitter because his travellers know what it ought to be like:

> 'Do you think,' asked Art, 'it might be the Green Isle of the Great Deep?'
> 'How could it be? because the Green Isle of the Great Deep is Paradise.'

That sort of idea, or mirage, lies behind the dream of islands.

6 The Might of the Sea

Na tuinn chaoirgheal mu Gharbhail,
neart na fairge 's a faram
Waves blazing with foam round Garvel, the might of the sea and its clangour.

George Campbell Hay

Walking on the machair above a long Atlantic beach, standing on rocks in spindrift like flying lace, lying awake like the poet, we recognise the power of the sea, even from the shore. And the sea, we know, can engulf the shore.

The interface between land and sea changes continually. If global warming continues, we're told, acres of coastline and flat land will be drowned. Acres have gone already over the years, submerged under water or blowing sand. At Skara Brae in Orkney one great gale buried a Stone Age village and another, centuries later, laid it bare again. The Culbin Sands on the Moray Firth still hide their secrets, but Andrew Young imagines what might come to light:

Here lay a fair fat land;
But now its townships, kirks, graveyards
Beneath bald hills of sand
Lie buried deep as Babylonian shards.

But gales may blow again;
And like a sand-glass turned about
The hills in a dry rain
Will flow away and the old land look out . . .

The rhythm of the sea – its moon-drawn tides, its rolling breakers with the legendary huge ninth wave – continues to fascinate writers. Andrew Murray Scott's second novel *Estuary Blue* has a strong water theme, considering the relationship between his home city Dundee and the Firth of Tay on which it lies, with sections titled 'Ebb-tide', 'Backwash', 'Tumbling Waters', 'Undertow' and 'Flood Tide'. But it's when you're out on the sea that it is most impressive, most dangerous, most invigorating. Seafaring poems have been written in Scotland since at least the eighteenth century, when the Gaelic poet Alasdair MacMhaighstir Alasdair described the stormy voyage of Birlinn Chlann Raghnaill, Clanranald's galley, from South Uist to Ireland. The translation here is by Iain Crichton Smith:

Na ceòsanaich àrda, chroma,
Teachd sa bhàirich;
Mun tigeadh iad idir nar caraibh,
Chluinnt' an gàirich;

Iad a' sguabadh nan tonn beaga
Lom gan sgiùrsadh.
Chinneadh i 'na h-aon mhuir bhàsmhor:
'S càs a stiùradh.

The wide-skirted curving waters,
bellowing, lowing,
before they even had approached you,
you'd hear roaring,

sweeping before them the small billows,
onward sheering.
There'd be a massive deathly water
hard for steering.

In good weather the sea is an exhilarating friend. On a clear day with a sweet wind, as George Campbell Hay conveys, you wouldn't want to be anywhere else. The singing rhythm becomes part of you and part of the poem:

Branches rocking, waves of shadow, all the trees
becked and swung in Glennan to the singing breeze,
Caisteal Aoil, the Brog, the Buck to leeward lay,
coming down the Kerry Shore at break of day.

Head on Tarbert, through the seas she raised a cry,
jewels of foam around her shoulders tossed on high,
green waves rose about her bows and broke away,
coming down the Kerry Shore at break of day.

But things can change without warning, and then your blood will freeze before the power of the sea. The Shetland poet 'Vagaland' saw the western waves. Perhaps he imagined them, or heard a returned sailor describe them; but it sounds like a real sighting, never to be forgotten, only to be exorcised in a poem:

> An sic a sicht A'm never seen!
> I tink I never will
> See onything laek dat agyin.
> Dey staand afore me still –
> Da tree graet waves in Papa Soond,
> Dir taps wi froadin white wis crooned,
> dir sides wis laek a hill!

These waves are discovered too by Neil Gunn's Caithness fishermen, in his novel *The Silver Darlings*, when they miss their landfall in the Hebrides and find themselves far out in the ocean:

> He had heard of a Gaelic poem that described all the different kinds of waves there
> are. But no poem could describe them all. Take this one coming at them now –
> now! – its water on the crest turned into little waters, running, herding together,
> before – up – up! over its shoulder and down into the long flecked hollow like a
> living skin. Or that one steaming off there! – a great lump of ocean, a long-backed
> ridge overtopping all, a piled-up mountain.

Seamen do not always live to describe the 'lump of water', the sudden freak wave which can overwhelm a boat in the blink of an eye. Since Viking times, and probably long before, poets, like seamen and their families, have known the sea as 'the widow-maker'. Helen B. Cruickshank's poem 'Overdue' is as bleak as grief:

> O ragin' wind
> An' cruel sea,
> Ye put the fear
> O' daith on me.
> I canna sleep,
> I canna pray,
> But prowl aboot
> The docks a' day,
> An' pu' my plaid
> Aboot me ticht,
> 'Nae news yet, mistress!' –
> *Ae mair nicht!*

The boats continued to go out. Fishing, which had been practised since the first people in Scotland settled on an inhospitable shore, gradually became a way of life and a source of traditional stories and rhymes:

> I cast my line in Largo Bay
> And fishes I caught nine:
> Three to boil and three to fry
> And three to bait the line.
> O weel may the boatie row
> And better may she speed;
> And weel may the boatie row
> That wins the bairnies' breid.

Eventually it became an organised industry, yet always dependent on the vagaries of weather, sea and fish. From the flourishing days of the herring fleets, before the First World War, we may note the light-hearted axiom of Neil Munro's character Para Handy: 'The herrin' iss a great, great mystery. The more you will be catchin' of them the more there iss; and when they're no' in't at aal they're no' there.' The shoals of fish moved in their season from the Minch in the west, north to Shetland and Caithness, south to East Anglia, and these movements were followed by boats and fishermen, merchants, curers, and the girls who gutted the herring and packed them in salt, their fingers protected by cotton bandages. Iain Crichton Smith's mother was one of those travelling fisher-lassies:

> You were gutting herring in distant Yarmouth and the salt sun in the morning
> rising out of the sea, the blood on the edge of your knife, and that salt so coarse
> that it stopped you from speaking and made your lips bitter.

Derick Thomson too acknowledges Clann-Nighean an Sgadain, 'the herring girls':

> An gàire mar chraiteachan salainn
> ga fhroiseadh bho 'm bheul,
> an sàl 's am picil air an teanga,
> 's na miaran cruinne, goirid a dheanadh giullachd,
> no a thogadh leanabh gu socair, cuimir,
> seasgair, fallain,
> gun mhearachd,
> 's na sùilean cho domhainn ri fèath.

> Their laughter like a sprinkling of salt
> showered from their lips,
> brine and pickle on their tongues,
> and the stubby short fingers that could handle fish,
> or lift a child gently, neatly,
> safely, wholesomely,
> unerringly,
> and the eyes that were deep as a calm.

Fishing communities grew up along the east and west and north coasts – Anstruther and Pittenweem, Fraserburgh and Peterhead, Tarbert and Mallaig – devoted to a hard and specialised way of life, developing a character of their own. John MacDougall Hay, brought up in Tarbert on Loch Fyne towards the end of the nineteenth century, set his novel *Gillespie* in a little town he calls 'Brieston', clearly recognisable as Tarbert. The fishing fleet of his time features in the book, in hard times, in storm, and in a great set-piece scene when the fleet, lying at anchor in the harbour, is set on fire:

> The anchor chains were red hot; spars crackled like musketry and hissed in
> the sea. Stars seemed falling from heaven. The wall of flame swayed and bent,
> and fell across the boats like gigantic flowers. The Harbour was a sea of fire;
> the tide like blood.

John MacDougall Hay moved away from Tarbert before his early death, but his son, who became the poet George Campbell Hay, often went back to visit relations there. He has memorably added to the picture of Tarbert and its fishermen:

> Calum thonder, long's the night to your thinking,
> night long till dawn and the sun set at the tiller,
> age and the cares of four and a boat to keep you
> high in the stern, alone for the winds to weary . . .

During his time the fishing industry fell on hard times and the fleets were much reduced. One of the last of the herring boats from upper Loch Fyne, *Sireadh* – which means 'Seeking' – became the central character in George Campbell Hay's poem 'Seeker, Reaper'. During much of the poem we are listening to her own voice. She speaks, or sings, in Old Norse and Gaelic as well as in Scots. She remembers the headlands she has rounded,

the reefs she has escaped, the harbours she has visited, though she isn't ready to settle down in harbour yet. We return to describing her action and her spirit:

> She's stieve, thrawn, light, quick,
> fast, wild, gay;
> she'll curtain the world wi hammered seas,
> she'll drench the stars wi spray.
> They can tower between her and the sky –
> she never felt their awe;
> she'll walk them aa, thon trampin' boat,
> she'll rise and walk them aa.
> She's a solan's hert, a solan's look;
> she canna thole a lee.
> I'll coil her ropes and redd her nets,
> and ease her through a sea.
> She's a seeker, she's a hawk, boys.
> Thon's the boat for me.

Meanwhile the ring-net fishing in Loch Fyne just after the Second World War was precisely and lovingly documented by Naomi Mitchison, collaborating with a Carradale fisherman, Denis Macintosh, in *Men and Herring*, which follows a crew from 'Port Fada' (Carradale) through a week at the fishing, with hard labour and jokes and quarrels and stewed tea; poor fishing to begin with, but then the tide turns:

> And at last they saw the green colour, like a field, of the herring below in the net,
> maybe two fathoms down, and someone cried, 'There they are, green!' And then
> in the next five minutes they had them right up, boiling up and into the wings,
> like chaff, spreading out for a width of four fathoms, all the space between the
> boats, and still two fathoms deep of them, all living and moving, and with a
> great strength in them.

And the startling beauty sometimes found in fishing-boat names has been used by Ian Hamilton Finlay in 'found poems':

> Green Waters
> Blue Spray
> Grayfish

Anna T
Karen B
Netta Croan

Constant Star
Daystar
Starwood

Starlit Waters
Moonlit Waters
Drift

Around Scotland's coasts, guiding the fishing-boats and all the other shipping, stand over eighty major lighthouses and many more minor lights. By now they are so much a part of the seascape that it's hard to realise they are a creation of, at most, the last 250 years. Before that, dangerous reefs were signalled by beacons of coal-fires or candles. Shipwrecks were so common that some shore-dwellers came to count on them as a source of household goods (it wasn't unknown for 'wreckers' to build a beacon in the wrong place, steering a ship towards, not away from, the rocks), and Walter Scott noticed, cruising around Scotland in 1814 on the lighthouse yacht *Pharos*, that not everybody was enthusiastic about lighthouses:

> Mr Stevenson happened to observe that the boat of a Sanday farmer had bad sails.
> 'If it had been [God's] will that you hadna built sae many lighthouses hereabout,'
> answered the Orcadian with great composure, 'I would have had new sails last winter.'

Robert Stevenson, Scott's companion on the *Pharos* expedition, was the head of a family who turned out to be remarkable in both lighthouses and literature. Robert himself built the Bell Rock lighthouse off the east coast of Scotland, on the reef previously marked only by the Inchcape Bell, and notable for the nineteenth-century poem by Robert Southey which tells how a pirate stole the bell:

> They hear no sound, the swell is strong,
> Though the wind hath fallen they drift along,
> Till the vessel strikes with a shivering shock –
> 'Oh Christ! it is the Inchcape Rock!'

Three of Robert Stevenson's sons followed him as lighthouse engineers, building remote Skerryvore south-west of Tiree, Muckle Flugga in Shetland, and Dubh Artach, off Mull. It was hoped that the dynasty would continue in a grandson, another Robert, but the young man had more interesting things on his mind, and we know him as the writer Robert Louis Stevenson.

R. L. S. readily acknowledged his engineering heritage. 'Whenever I smell salt water,' he wrote, 'I know I am not far from one of the works of my ancestors.' He named his house in Bournemouth 'Skerryvore', explaining why:

> For love of lovely words, and for the sake
> Of those, my kinsmen and my countrymen,
> Who early and late in the windy ocean toiled
> To plant a star for seamen, where was then
> The surfy haunt of seals and cormorants . . .

And his brief apprenticeship – he did spend some time on site as an observer – left other marks in his work. In his novel *Kidnapped*, the Torran Rocks off the coast of Mull (now signalled by the light of Dubh Artach, which R. L. S. saw under construction) bring disaster to the brig *Covenant*:

> The tide caught the brig, and threw the wind out of her sails. She came round
> into the wind like a top, and the next moment struck the reef with such a dunch
> as threw us all flat upon the deck . . . Sometimes the swell broke clean over us;
> sometimes it only ground the poor brig upon the reef, so that we could hear her
> beat herself to pieces . . .

After the shipwreck David Balfour spends four miserable days on the island of Erraid with nothing to eat but raw shellfish, while passing fisherman laugh at him because he doesn't know that he could leave at low tide, 'dry-shod, or at the least by wading'. Stevenson has picked up this local information, almost certainly during his tour of duty at Dubh Artach, and he uses his observations to even greater effect in his story 'The Merry Men'. These are fifty-foot breakers which get their name from their wild dancing, or perhaps, the narrator muses, 'from the shouting they make about the turn of the tide':

The night, though we were so little past midsummer, was as dark as January . . .
Sheets of mingled spray and rain were driven in our faces. All round the isle of
Aros the surf, with an incessant hammering thunder, beat upon the reefs and
beaches. Now louder in one place, now lower in another, like the combinations
of orchestral music, the constant mass of sound hardly varied for a moment.
And loud above all this hurly-burly I could hear the changeful voice of the
Roost and the intermittent roaring of the Merry Men.

For some years now all Scotland's lighthouses have been automated and keepers are no longer employed.
Theirs was not a solitary job, since each light was always staffed with three men in case of illness or sudden
death, and for long periods at a time it must have seemed more boring than dangerous, but there was
danger too. To this day no one knows what happened to the three keepers of the Flannan Isles light, two
hundred miles west of Lewis. The light was reported to be out and a relief ship sent to investigate found no
sign of life. Entries in the log-book stopped a week before, but nothing unusual had been noted. The lamp had
been trimmed and the house was tidy. The poet Wilfrid Wilson Gibson wrote about the mystery, adding a few
Marie Celeste-like details of his own:

> Like curs a glance has brought to heel
> We listened, flinching there:
> And looked, and looked, on the untouched meal,
> And the overtoppled chair.
>
> We seemed to stand for an endless while,
> Though still no word was said,
> Three men alive on Flannan Isle,
> Who thought on three men dead.

Though many theories for the disappearance were put forward – madness, sea-serpents, a curse on the
light – some signs of storm damage at the west landing-place suggested a simpler explanation. Experienced
and safety-conscious as they were, the men were swept to their death by the unpredictable, irresistible power
of the sea.

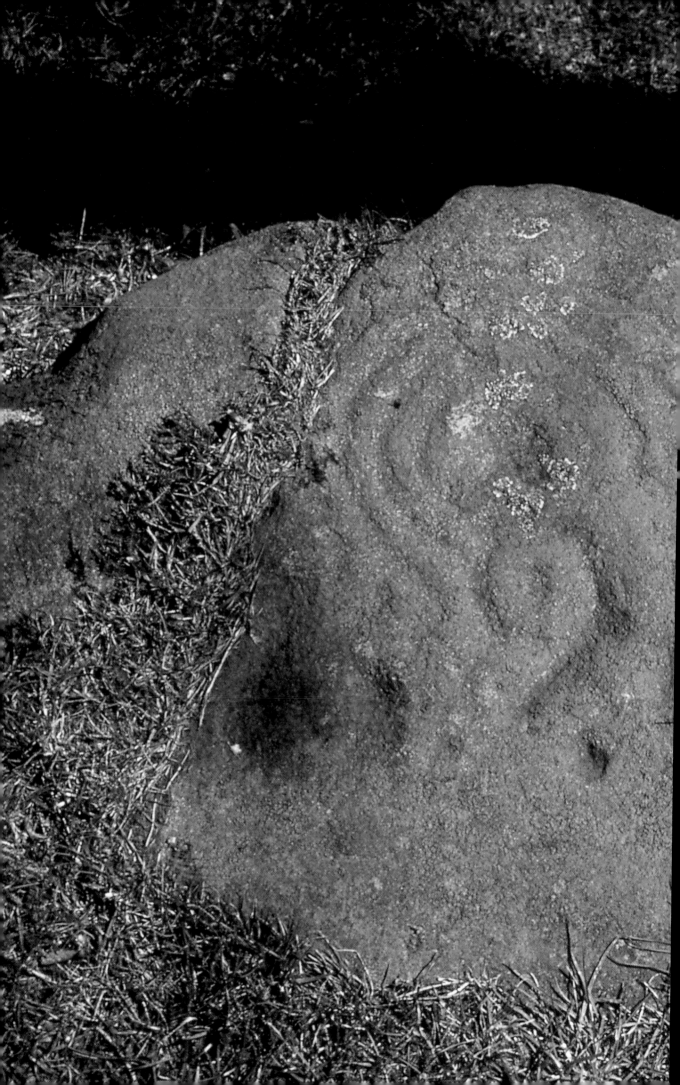

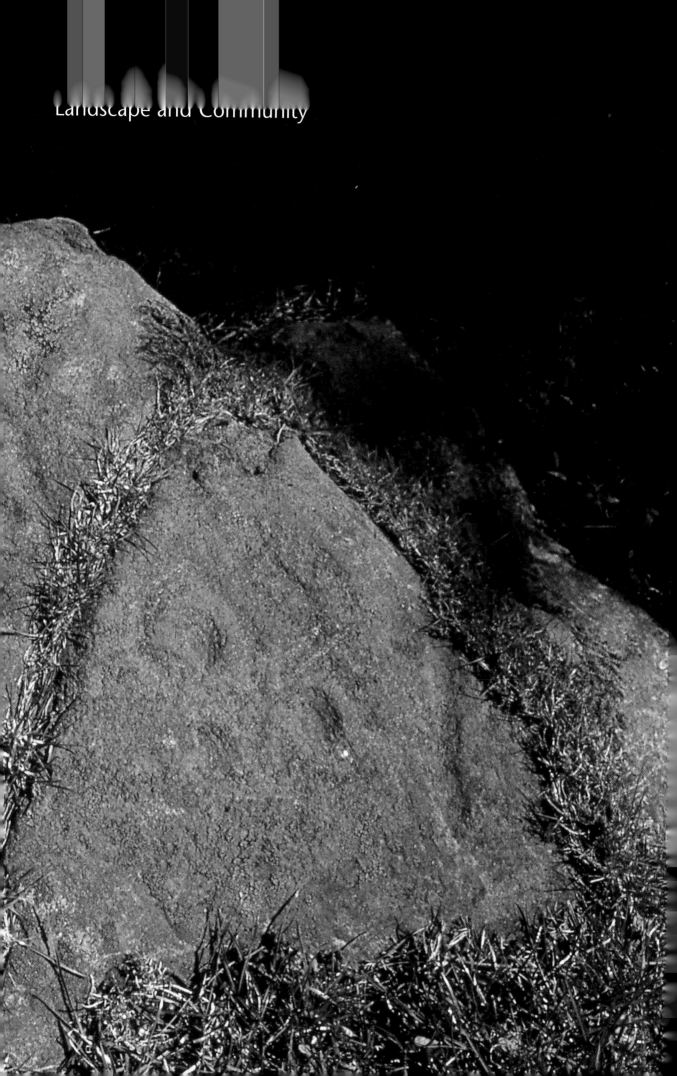

7 Stone and Spire

The kirk, in a gale of psalms, went heaving through
A tumult of roofs, freighted for heaven.

George Mackay Brown

The landscape of Scotland is marked with standing stones, grey witnesses whose history and purpose is unclear. The great stone circles like Callanish in Lewis and Brodgar in Orkney are each part of a sacred landscape in which the elements of stones and mounds have been carefully sited. The circle by Blawearie Loch, in Lewis Grassic Gibbon's fictional version of the Mearns, is a constant presence throughout *A Scots Quair*:

> Nearby the bit loch was a circle of stones from olden times, some were upright
> and some were flat and some leaned this way and that, and right in the middle
> three big ones clambered up out of the earth and stood askew with flat sonsy faces,
> they seemed to listen and wait. They were Druid stones and folk told that the
> Druids had been coarse devils of men in the times long syne, they'd climb up
> there and sing their foul heathen songs around the stones; and if they met a
> bit Christian missionary they'd gut him as soon as look at him.

Perhaps it wasn't quite like that, and perhaps they aren't 'Druid stones', but there's probably a grain of truth in the perception of the folk. The first people of Scotland had holy places, which may still be holy today.

We can trace some of these sites, and not only where stones remain. All over the map are place-names which give us a clue. There's a belief in Cromarty that the Last Judgment will take place on the moor of Navity. That's because the name Navity, like Rosneath in Dunbartonshire and Duneaves in Perthshire, comes from *nemeton*, which – in France and Ireland as well as in Scotland – signifies a holy place of great antiquity. These were pagan shrines later taken over by the Christian church. There's a tradition that St Columba found druids before him on the island of Iona, and it has been suggested that the original form of the name Iona may have meant 'place of the yew tree', a tree sacred to the druids.

We can look near the place-name Annat (or something derived from it, like Craigannet in Stirlingshire or Annaty Burn near Scone in Perthshire) for traces of an early church or burial ground. Often there's a well or a stream, which in pre-Christian times would have had its god or spirit. 'The wine of the burn of the Annat,' says Duncan Ban Macintyre, the poet of Ben Dorain, 'its taste was of honey to drink it.'

It's well known that names beginning with 'kil' mark the location of a chapel or the cell of a missionary saint, so that Kilkerran – a name found in both Ayrshire and Kintyre – was the cell of St Kieran, and Kilmuir, frequently found, was dedicated to the Virgin Mary. Some of the early churches are now only ruined walls, standing beside burying-grounds with Celtic interlacing on the old carved stones. Traces of their past seem to linger around

them, as Neil Gunn suggests in *The Silver Darlings*. His characters, walking up Dunbeath Strath in Caithness, come upon a tumble of stones, 'a grey-blue softened with lichen'. Catrine asks Roddie what it is:

> 'The old folk call it Chapelhill,' he answered. 'It seems there was a church here
> at one time, though I have heard it said that long, long ago it was a monastery
> and the name it had was the House of Peace.'
>
> 'The House of Peace,' she murmured in a tone of wonder.
>
> He gave her a side glance and smiled. 'You like that name?'
>
> 'Yes,' she answered, confused slightly, for the name had been like a benediction
> sounded softly in her mind.

As the missionary saints made use of the pagan traditions they found, so their followers benefited from the reputation of the original small churches, extending and rebuilding on the same sites, so that some holy places have remained powerhouses of faith through the years. St Ninian's at Whithorn and St Cuthbert's in Edinburgh, for instance, are directly descended, it is thought, from their founding saints. When still larger buildings were demanded by population changes and church politics, the best masons and woodcarvers of the medieval world were employed to demonstrate the glory of God (and the wealth of the Church). Walter Scott appreciated the beauty of the Border abbeys, Dryburgh, Jedburgh, Kelso and Melrose, though they were long ruined even by his time:

> If thou would'st view fair Melrose aright,
> Go visit it by the pale moonlight . . .
> When the broken arches are black in night,
> And each shafted oriel glimmers white;
> When the cold light's uncertain shower
> Streams on the ruin'd central tower;
> When buttress and buttress, alternately,
> Seem fram'd of ebon and ivory . . .

Scott often took visitors to see Melrose, though he admitted later that he had never in fact seen it by moonlight when he wrote these famous lines. But that's what a poet's imagination is for.

While many Scottish churches were destroyed or abandoned at the time of the Reformation in the sixteenth century, some are still in use. Glasgow Cathedral, as Scott knew, is one of these. His character Andrew Fairservice in *Rob Roy* relates how the citizens of Glasgow defended the building against the zeal of the reformers – a heartwarming tale, even if probably not true – so that 'the auld kirk stood as crouse as a cat when the flaes are kaimed aff her and a'body was alike pleased'. We may now regret the loss of some of the fleas, the medieval statues and such ornamentation, but the Cathedral does survive as Andrew describes it:

> . . . a brave kirk – nane o' yere whigmaleeries and curliewurlies and open-steek
> hems about it – a' solid, weel-jointed mason-wark, that will stand as lang as the
> warld, keep hands and gunpowther aff it.

It has always been something for tourists – including visiting writers – to see. Robert Southey, poet laureate in the early nineteenth century, wasn't impressed: 'The seats are so closely packed that any person who would remain there during the time of service must have an invincible nose.' A few years, later Harriet Beecher Stowe, author of *Uncle Tom's Cabin* and forerunner of the American tourist trade, admitted that she was overtired when she saw it: 'I could hardly walk through the building . . . Nothing is so utterly hazardous to a person's strength as looking at cathedrals'.

But the powerful grouping of Cathedral and Necropolis shows up in the work of many writers about Glasgow. The troubled mind of a character in John Galt's *The Entail* is reflected in the eerie scene:

> The clouds were rolling in black and lowering masses, through which an
> occasional gleam of sunshine flickered for a moment on the towers and pinnacles
> of the cathedral, and glimmered in its rapid transit on the monuments and graves
> in the churchyard . . . The gusty wind howled like a death dog among the firs,
> which waved their dark boughs like hearse plumes over him.

And both Cathedral and Necropolis have important roles in Alasdair Gray's novel *Lanark*, set partly in Glasgow and partly in the fantastic cities of Unthank and Provan, which are (perhaps) aspects of a nightmarish future Glasgow. It is from the Necropolis that the main character Lanark descends into the sinister Institute. Later he finds that the Cathedral is now Unthank's centre of government, though still recognisable: 'a sturdy Gothic ark, the sculpted waterspouts broken and rubbed by weather and the hammers of old iconoclasts'. In an apocalyptic last chapter we see 'the whole landscape tilted like a board' as subsidence and flood threaten the Cathedral, but it survives.

Kirkwall Cathedral in Orkney, another Scottish pre-Reformation cathedral still in use, is dedicated to St Magnus the Martyr. As recently as 1919, when the interior of the cathedral was being restored, workmen found an oaken chest containing a skull with a gaping axe-wound. According to the *Orkneyinga Saga*, that was how Magnus, Earl of Orkney, met his death. The bones were sealed up again in one of the great red sandstone pillars, though 'Mansie's Kist' (Magnus's chest) can be seen in the local museum. The story with all its resonances lies at the heart of George Mackay Brown's poetry and fiction:

> The Magnustide long swords of rain
> Quicken the dust. The ploughman turns
> Furrow by holy furrow
> The liturgy of April.

Arbuthnott Kirk in the Mearns is a pre-Reformation parish church. It would be easy for the tourist to miss, but it is as important to Scottish literature as any cathedral, because it features, as the kirk of Kinraddie, in Lewis Grassic Gibbon's *Sunset Song*:

> Hidden away among these yews were kirk and manse. Next door the kirk was an
> old tower, built in the time of the Roman Catholics, the coarse creatures, and it
> was fell old and wasn't used any more except by the cushat-doves and they flew
> in and out the narrow slits in the upper storey and nested all the year round and
> the place was fair white with their dung. In the lower half of the tower was an
> effigy-thing of Cospatrick de Gondeshil, him that killed the gryphon, lying on
> his back with his arms crossed and a daft-like simper on his face.

Gibbon was brought up in the Mearns, and, though he died in London, his ashes were interred in Arbuthnott kirkyard. Helen B. Cruickshank attended the ceremony on a cold day of early spring:

> Clouds of smoke on the hill
> where the whin is burning,
> staining the clear cold sky
> as the sun goes down.
> Brighter the fire leaps up
> as night grows darker;
> wild and lovely the light
> of the flaming whin . . .

This man set the flame
of his native genius
under the cumbering whin
of the untilled field;
Lit a fire in the Mearns
to illumine Scotland,
clearing the sullen soil
for a richer yield.

After the Reformation came the distinctive sober stone parish churches so familiar in Scottish towns. (From years of disruption, re-unification and further secession, one town may have many church buildings.) They have made their way into bairn-rhymes and finger-games:

Here's the church and here's the steeple;
Open the door and there's the people.
Here's the minister climbing upstairs,
And here's the minister saying his prayers.

The rhyme is illustrated by linking the fingers until the thumb is waggling vigorously inside a pulpit-rail, like the minister 'waggin' his pow in a pulpit', traditionally the dearest ambition of the poor Scottish mother for her bright boy. Burns observed the ministers with his customary sardonic eye, including the one in 'The Holy Fair' who carries out the pow-wagging with such zeal:

Hear how he clears the points o' Faith
Wi' rattlin an' thumpin!
Now meekly calm, now wild in wrath,
He's stampan, an' he's jumpan!

The church was part of the townscape even for those bright boys whose talents turned more to poetry than to preaching. In eighteenth-century Edinburgh Robert Fergusson sees the beauty of the scene when 'morn, with bonnie purpie-smiles' – that is, blushes – 'kisses the air-cock o' Saint Giles'. Though he addresses the discordant Tron Kirk bell in humorous exasperation:

> Wanwordy, crazy, dinsome thing,
> As e'er was fram'd to jow or ring,
> What gar'd them sic in steeple hing
>   They ken themsel',
> But weel wat I they coudna bring
>   Waur sounds frae hell.

Nearly two centuries later, looking at the long skyline of the Royal Mile, Lewis Spence sees only the beauty, which in some lights truly seems from another world:

> Pillar to pillar, stane to stane,
> The cruikit spell o' her backbane,
> Yon shadow-mile o' spire and vane,
> Wad ding them a', wad ding them a'!

Scottish poets, in fact, are quite impressed by the architecture of their churches. Moreover they like the high-jinks at the fairs which used to be held in the church grounds. A medieval poet, who may have been one of Scotland's cultured Stewart kings, enjoyed describing the excited girls who 'squealed like any gaits, full loud' at the dancing on such a festive day 'at Christ's Kirk on the green'. And Burns took up the theme in 'The Holy Fair':

> How monie hearts this day converts,
> O' Sinners and o' Lasses!
> Their hearts o' stane gin night are gane
> As saft as ony flesh is.
> There's some are fou o' love divine,
> There's some are fou o' brandy;
> An' monie jobs that day begin
> May end in houghmagandie
>   Some ither day.

As to what goes on inside the kirk, poets sometimes observe that with a cooler eye. Scotland used to be a famously Sabbath-observing nation, but in spite of that (or perhaps because of it) the perceptions poets have of ministers tend to be less than favourable. Tom Scott, like others, blames the Reformation:

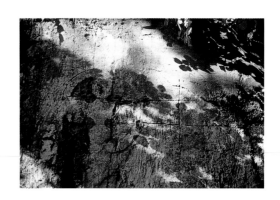

They made His day a rookery o kirks,
His pulpit nests o craws,
And lowsed on us a herd o lowan stirks
Wi iron hoofs and jaws . . .

As for churchgoers, they're scary, as Hugh MacDiarmid suggests:

Oh to be at Crowdieknowe
When the last trump blaws,
An' see the deid come loupin' owre
The auld grey wa's.

Muckle men wi' tousled beards
I grat at as a bairn
'll scramble frae the croodit clay
Wi' feck o' swearin'.

An' glower at God an' a' his gang
O' angels i' the lift
– Thae trashy bleezin' French-like folk
Wha gar'd them shift!

Fain the weemun-folk'll seek
To mak' them haud their row
– Fegs, God's no blate gin he stirs up
The men o' Crowdieknowe!

Or they're hypocritical, like Burns's Holy Willie:

But Lord, remember me and mine
Wi' mercies temporal and divine!
That I for grace and gear may shine,
      Excell'd by nane!
And a' the glory shall be thine!
      Amen! Amen!

Violet Jacob takes a much gentler view of the churchgoer who is there in body but not entirely in spirit. 'When a'body's thochts is set on their ain salvation', her young Tam addresses his Jean, 'mine's set on you.'

Here and there we do tap into something deeper: the reason the churches are there. Very deep, perhaps, are the mysteries of Rosslyn Chapel in Midlothian. Scott made use of its legends and atmosphere:

> Seem'd all on fire that chapel proud
> Where Roslin's chiefs uncoffin'd lie,
> Each Baron, for a sable shroud,
> Sheath'd in his iron panoply.
>
> Seem'd all on fire, within, around,
> Deep sacristy and altar's pale;
> Shone every pillar foliage-bound,
> And glimmer'd all the dead men's mail.

It even provides a set-piece in Ian Rankin's crime novel *Set in Darkness*. The young detective sergeant is duly impressed:

> The interior was as ornate as any cathedral's, its scale serving to heighten the effect
> of the stonework. The vaulted ceiling boasted carvings of different kinds of flowers.
> There were intricate pillars and stained-glass windows . . .

The Prentice Pillar was carved by a young apprentice whose master, jealous of the boy's skill, killed him with a mallet-blow (though it's true to say that there are similar legends in other great churches, like Lincoln and Rouen.) The riot of carvings includes angels, gospel stories and medieval allegories – and pagan symbols – worked by master-craftsmen whose names are unknown. Strangest of all, some of the plants recognisable in the carvings are native to America, which had not yet been discovered when the chapel was built. At least, it hadn't been discovered by Columbus. There's a strong tradition that a member of the Sinclair family – 'the lordly line of high St Clair' who built the chapel – got to the New World first.

However, none of this cuts much ice with Rankin's hero Inspector Rebus. The foundation stone of the chapel was laid in 1446, and building continued for nearly forty years. 'Sounds like some builders I know,' Rebus observes. And he's rather dismissive about the secrets it may hide. 'This is where the spaceship is, eh?' But as strong as the belief in the Loch Ness Monster is the belief that there's something extremely secret beneath the floor of Rosslyn Chapel. Some say this is the resting-place of the Holy Grail.

8 The Life of the Land

This is my country,
The land that begat me.
These windy spaces
Are surely my own.

Alexander Gray

When John Keats, like a good literary tourist, visited the Burns country of Ayrshire in 1818, he was pleasantly surprised. He had pictured it as desolate, but 'O prejudice!' he wrote, 'it was as rich as Devon'. It's true that the month was July, and Keats was just passing through. Burns himself, familiar with his countryside in every month of the year and every kind of weather, could have supplied a different picture. His ploughman's collie Luath in 'The Twa Dogs' tersely describes the farmworker 'howckan in a sheugh'. 'Digging in a ditch' is the nearest English phrase, except that a sheugh is much muddier than a ditch, full of clabber and glaur.

Country life is a recurring theme for Scottish writers, with these two contrasting perceptions – rich and beggarly – jostling for place. Hugh MacDiarmid closely observes the well-farmed acres of East Lothian:

> Across the heavy-laden grainfields;
> Over the great broad rectangles of potato land,
> Thigh deep in their dark green covering of shaughs:
> Beyond the flickering blue-green tops of the thickly-clustering swedes,
> Or the paler pastures, where heavy Border Leicesters
> Or their crosses are lazily grazing the rye grass and clover ley
> And tramping it hard for the autumn ploughing . . .

Flora Garry, brought up in the agricultural heartland of Buchan, knows that the path from a heavy-laden grainfield to harvest isn't always straightforward:

> She promised weel aneuch – a heavy crap.
> Bit a dull, mochy Simmer it wis, wi afa little drooth.
> Some o's, ye'll min', gey forcey, cuttit ower green,
> An syne the widder broke.

Still there's a pervasive dream of a rural paradise. Perhaps it comes from a memory of the shielings, the high pastures where the cattle of the Highlands were driven in early summer, partly to make the most of the upland grazing, partly to keep the beasts out of the crops below. Generally it was the women and children of the settlement who stayed with the cattle, knitting and spinning and making butter and cheese, through the long light days and scarcely-dark nights. Even Burns knew the gentle lilt of the traditional song 'Crodh Chailein', Colin's cattle:

A maiden sang sweetly
As bird on a tree,
Cro' Chailean, Cro' Chailean,
Cro' Chailean for me.

In the morning they wander
To their pastures afar,
Where the grass grows the greenest
By corrie and scaur . . .

We can be sure of this because the social club where he spent evenings in Edinburgh took its name, the Crochallan Fencibles, from the song, a favourite of one of the club's leading lights.

Perhaps the dream grew even stronger as more and more of the population of Scotland, for various reasons, turned from the land to live in towns. Robert McLellan, remembering his childhood holidays in Clydesdale, sees how this can be:

I had been born there, my minnie said, and I wad hae been gled neir to hae left it,
but that couldna be. My faither had his business in a toun. It's queer that I can
hardly mind a haet aboot the toun whaur I bade in my bairnhood, whan I can
mind ilka blade o the Linmill grass.

Many wandering Scots had the same sort of memories. Charles Murray spent his working life in South Africa early in the twentieth century, but made many visits home to Aberdeenshire, and his poetry evokes his native countryside in its own rich tongue. (More often than not he is referred to as 'Hamewith' – 'homewards' – the title of one poem.) His pictures of the golden age, like 'The Whistle', attained great popularity both at home and abroad:

He cut a sappy sucker from the muckle rodden-tree,
He trimmed it, an' he wet it, an' he thumped it on his knee;
He never heard the teuchat when the harrow broke her eggs,
He missed the craggit heron nabbin' puddocks in the seggs,
He forgot to hound the collie at the cattle when they strayed,
But you should hae seen the whistle that the wee herd made! . . .

> He blew them rants sae lively, schottisches, reels, an' jigs,
> The foalie flang his muckle legs an' capered ower the rigs,
> The grey-tailed futt'ratt bobbit oot to hear his ain strathspey,
> The bawd cam' loupin' through the corn to 'Clean Pease Strae';
> The feet o' ilka man an' beast gat youkie when he played –
> Hae ye ever heard o' whistle like the wee herd made?

Yet Murray was quite aware of a dark side to the idyll. Even for the laddie in 'The Whistle', reality had to break in. By law he had to go to school, not then or now the most hospitable of environments for a musician and dreamer, and there 'the maister brunt the whistle that the wee herd made'. And Murray completely demolishes the genial façade of the well-doing Buchan farmer in his brilliant poem 'Dockens Afore his Peers', as sharply observed and satirical as 'Holy Willie's Prayer'. It is 1916 and the farmer is working hard to convince a tribunal of his neighbours that none of his family or workforce should be called up for war service. His younger son is clearly eligible for the draft, so a few favours have to be called in:

> Hoot, Mains, hae mind, I'm doon for you some sma' thing wi' the bank;
> Aul' Larickleys, I saw you throu', an' this is a' my thank;
> An' Gutteryloan, that time ye broke, to Dockenhill ye cam' –
> 'Total exemption.' Thank ye, sirs. Fat say ye till a dram?

Country people, indeed, have always known that rural life is no bed of roses. Farmworkers in north-east Scotland were fee'd – employed for a short time only – finding their next position at the regular feeing fairs or markets. There, a young man might be tempted by the proffered chance of working with a splendid pair of horses, only to find that the farmer had exaggerated a bit:

> I gaed in by Turra market,
> Turra market for to fee,
> I fell in wi' a farmer chiel
> Frae the Barnyards o' Delgaty.
>
> He promised me the ae best pair
> I ever set my e'en upon;
> When I gaed hame to the Barnyards
> There was naething there but skin and bone.

From the rough and ready bunkhouses for unmarried workers, known as chaumers or bothies, came these bothy ballads, harsh, humorous and lyrical at the same time:

> There's a fairm up in Cairnie
> That's kent baith faur and wide
> Tae be the great Drumdelgie
> Upon sweet Deveronside.
> The fairmer o' yon muckle toun
> He is baith hard and sair,
> And the cauldest day that ever blaws,
> His servants get their share.

This strictly non-idyllic view is the one most often taken by Scottish writers now. David Toulmin knows all about it, since he went into service as an orra loon – the odd-job boy about the farm – at the age of fourteen. His short stories set on Buchan farms have room for both the beauty and the hardness of country life, and, like his novel *Blown Seed*, are fairly outspoken about country matters. Here he's writing about the annual Aikey Fair:

> You could look at the beauty of your quine against the pine trees and the
> pale summer sky. But you weren't yourselves, for there were a lot of other
> couples on the brae, kissing and cuddling and having a carry-on . . .
> for Aikey was famed for its brazen courting on the hillside, and the quines
> who lost their knickers among the whins.

Duncan McLean, brought up in the same area, brings country life up to date in his novel *Blackden*. His character Paddy Hunter is an auctioneer's apprentice, and if we suspect that the old farming way of life may be on its way out, Paddy can confirm that, because he's selling it off piece by piece: 'a hosepipe and stirrup-pump; a wooden plunge-kirn, its staves dried out and loosened; a roll of barbed wire; a set of riddles; a rusty neep-hasher . . .' Not that Paddy cares, because as soon as he can he's out of there:

> Below me and half a mile to my right was a small farm with a straggle of
> outbuildings and a long narrow track leading down into the trees at the denside.
> Goodman's Croft! I was back there again! That was the problem with this part of
> the world, this hollow in the hills: if you didn't watch out you'd spend your whole
> life whizzing round and round the walls of the den like a motorbiker on a wall of
> death. Going a hell of a speed, maybe, but never actually getting anywhere.

Paddy knows there's a life beyond the farm, he's ready to embrace it, and, because he's a thoroughly modern country boy, there's every chance that he will succeed. It wasn't always so easy. Burns, farming in Ayrshire and Dumfriesshire, left it too late, and his health was ruined by the time he gave up on the thin soil of Ellisland, writing to his brother 'This farm has undone my enjoyment of myself'. James Hogg, 'the Ettrick Shepherd', was in fact something of an authority on the problems of sheep. Even as a friend of Scott and a literary tourist, old habits died hard: 'Consulting several tours through Scotland,' he wrote sternly, 'I found in none of them any observations on the great neglect of sheep-stock.' But he was far better at writing than at agriculture, and when he became a farmer on his own account at Altrive Lake and Mount Benger in the Borders, he struggled long and hard.

Farming life was a round of ceaseless labour. Both men and women found themselves harnessed to the plough, or its equivalent. Charles Murray's Dockens is offhand enough about his kitchenmaid's duties:

> Weel, syne we hae the kitchie deem, that milks an' mak's the maet,
> She disna aft haud doon the deese, she's at it ear' an' late,
> She cairries seed, an' braks the muck, an' gies a han' to hyow,
> An' churns, an' bakes, an' syes the so'ens, an' fyles there's peats to rowe.

We don't, however, learn how the kitchie deem regarded all this. Flora Garry, brought up in the same north-east farming country, sees a young woman torn by opposing forces. It's a beautiful place and her home is there, but she feels tethered to Bennygoak, 'the hill of the cuckoo':

> I look far ower by Ythanside
> To Fyvie's laich, lythe laans,
> To Auchterless an Bennachie
> An the mist-blue Grampians.
> Sair't o the hull o Bennygoak
> An scunnert o the ferm,
> Gin I bit daar't, gin I bit daar't,
> I'd flit the comin term . . .

'Flit, flit, ye feel,' says the unco bird,
'There's finer, couthier folk
An kinlier country hine awaa
Fae the hull o Bennygoak.'
Bit ma midder's growein aal an deen
An likes her ain fireside.
Twid brak her hert to leave the hull:
It's brakkin mine to bide.

These opposing forces are overwhelmingly at work in Lewis Grassic Gibbon's great novel *Sunset Song*. Chris Guthrie grows up with the harshness and cruelty and hard work of the farm. At times she hates it all, and for her there's a way out, since she's clever at school, encouraged by her teacher to go on to higher education. She imagines herself away from 'the weary pleiter of the land', at university, becoming a teacher, with a house of her own. How glad she'll be! Or maybe she won't. 'Two Chrisses there were that fought for her heart and tormented her,' as one day she hates the land, and the next day knows it's part of her.

When her father dies and there's money to go away, to build a new life, she walks over the fields to bring in the cattle, thinking about all she's going to do:

> And then a queer thought came to her there in the drooked fields, that nothing
> endured at all, nothing but the land she passed across, tossed and turned and
> perpetually changed below the hands of the crofter folk since the oldest of them
> had set the Standing Stones by the loch of Blawearie and climbed there on their
> holy days and saw their terraced crops ride brave in the wind and sun.

The land – that's what the little boy of Linmill remembers. Even if Paddy at the auctioneer's sells off the plough and the tractor, their marks are still in the soil and the land is still there.

Jessie Kesson in her farming novel *Glitter of Mica* brings that sharply before her central character:

> . . . one morning on his road to school he had stood arrested, staring at the sharp
> gleaming coulter of the plough cutting into the hill slope and leaving the first dark
> furrow. That had struck him with an almost physical sense of pain. And the image
> of the virgin land with the gash of a wound across it had lain unvoiced in mind for
> a long time.

The land remains, inextricably connected with the people who farm it, whether today or a hundred generations ago. In Grassic Gibbon's short story 'Clay' the farmer of Pittaulds, having worked himself nearly to death in his unforgiving fields, opens up a hole containing a skeleton, some flint tools, and something shaped like a heuch, a sickle or scythe. His daughter recognises the site as an 'earth-house', a prehistoric grave, but to the farmer it has a much more direct significance. 'Look at that heuch,' he says, 'it once scythed Pittaulds.' Thousands of years apart, he and his ancestor meet in the work of the land.

9 The Big House

Living in the Big House is being
The big stag, the twelve-pointer,
Watched on, edible, spied and lied to.

Naomi Mitchison

Wherever you go in Scotland you're likely to see a castle, a mansion, a big house, looming gaunt on a headland or screened behind trees. Sometimes it is still occupied as a family home, by its original owners or otherwise. Sometimes it's a ruin. Sometimes it has become a hotel; and sometimes, enhanced with noticeboards, a tearoom and a coach-park, it's a tourist attraction, set apart – nothing whatever to do, we may feel, with everyday Scotland at its gates.

Yet if we stand back and look at it, we see that it is part of the landscape, and not only in the artistic sense. It is there, on that particular spot, for a reason. Even if it's a newish mansion, it is quite likely shadowed by the ruined walls of an older house, which in its turn may have been built on a hillock which is now half-obliterated, but which, in earliest times, was a prime defensive site. The whole complex is part of the story of the land. Even if you dismiss it as irrelevant, as many Scottish writers do, the fact that it once was relevant is at the back of your mind.

To a few writers the big house may be part of their own lives. Carolina Oliphant, by marriage Lady Nairne, was born in the old House of Gask in Perthshire, in 1766, twenty years after the battle of Culloden which effectively ended Jacobite hopes. The Oliphant family was famously Jacobite, to the extent that Carolina was named after 'the King over the water', Bonnie Prince Charlie, and so were her brother Charles and sister Charlotte. As an adult she wrote the Jacobite songs 'Charlie is my Darling' and 'Will ye no' come back again?'. She also remembered her childhood home:

> Oh the auld hoose, the auld hoose,
> What though the rooms were wee,
> Oh, kind hearts were dwelling there,
> And bairnies fu' o' glee . . .
> The mavis still doth sweetly sing,
> The bluebells sweetly blaw,
> The bonnie Earn's clear winding still,
> But the auld hoose is awa'.

Another verse of 'The Auld Hoose' recalls how her mother and father once 'sheltered Scotland's heir'. Family and national history were inextricably entwined in Gask.

Elizabeth Grant spent part of her nineteenth-century childhood at her family home, the Doune of Rothiemurchus, which took its name from the hill at its back, once fortified and still retaining clear traces of a moat. Her uncle, the laird, had moved a few miles away and built a new house, but Elizabeth preferred the Doune:

> The old house had a few low rooms on the ground floor with many dark closets;
> the principal apartment was on the first floor, and reached by a wide and easy stair;
> the family bedroom was on the one hand, a large hall on the other for the
> reception of guests, and the state bedroom through it. Up in the atticks, beneath
> the steep grey roof, were little rooms again. This was the highland home to which
> my mother had been brought a Bride.

Walter Scott's ancestors were important men on the Borders and he preserved a romantic view of the way things used to be:

> He pass'd where Newark's stately tower
> Looks out from Yarrow's birchen bower:
> The Minstrel gazed with wishful eye –
> No humbler resting-place was nigh;
> With hesitating step at last
> The embattled portal arch he pass'd,
> Whose ponderous grate and massy bar
> Had oft roll'd back the tide of war,
> But never closed the iron door
> Against the desolate and poor.

By the time he was born, in the last quarter of the eighteenth century, his branch of the family no longer lived in such state, and his career was laid out for him not as a reiver but as a douce Edinburgh lawyer. But he made himself a laird, building Abbotsford, near Melrose, something of a time capsule even when it was new, and a lasting memorial to the romantic conception of the big house.

The trouble about this view of Scottish history is the rose-coloured shadow which it casts. The truth can be rather different. The Victorian hymn praises the status quo of 'the rich man in his castle, the poor man at his gate', but the poor man's gate was sometimes deemed to be rather too near the castle. While the planned towns and villages built in the eighteenth and nineteenth centuries generally aimed to improve employment and living conditions for the tenants, some were designed also to improve the landscape for the laird and his guests. The original villages, which had grown up like living things, were moved, people and all, some distance away. The results can be beautiful – Inveraray in Argyll with its white houses and arched pends, charming Houston in Renfrewshire with its old inn – but it's hard to forget how much it suited the proprietor to get those messy old cottages and their inhabitants out from under his feet. Much worse are the memories which cling around Scalloway Castle in Shetland, for, as Robert Alan Jamieson recalls, it was built for the wicked Earl Patrick Stewart by means of forced labour:

> Quhitever shite drappt oot dy privvies
> Still maer bed on ahint, inside de,
> In da trots an haas an guts
> O da Stewart clan at aaned de.
>
> I canna celebrate dy stonn in ony tongue
> Nor care tae rub da green fae yon bress plaet
> Da National Trust sae carefilly hae nailed ta de.
> Fir every chisel swap, a bairn gret oot fir maet . . .

And for every writer brought up in a stately home, there were, and still are, twenty who look at these seats of privilege with distinctly jaundiced eyes. We do occasionally find poets complimenting lords and lairds, but they may well be touting for patronage. That didn't always work out. We hear of the Kirkintilloch weaver poet Walter Watson who, as a young man at the end of the eighteenth century, rather fancied the life of a full-time bard supported by his local laird. In hope of sponsorship he took his poem 'The Braes o' Bedlay' up to the big house:

> Whaur Mary and I meet amang the green bushes,
> That screen us sae weel on the braes o' Bedlay . . .

Most unfortunately he'd forgotten that the braes of Bedlay were on the laird's land. Sponsorship? Forget it! He was thrown out as a trespasser, lucky to escape jail.

Even Burns, so independent and radical, obtained help from the Earl of Glencairn, thanked him in verse, and named a son after him. We may surmise that the bard was slightly tongue-in-cheek when he celebrated his acquaintanceship with another member of the aristocracy:

This wot all ye whom it concerns,
I, rhymer Rab, alias Burns,
          October twenty-third,
A ne'er to be forgotten day!
Sae far I sprachl'd up the brae,
          I dinner'd wi' a Lord.

But Burns was never in any danger of losing his sense of proportion ('Ye see yon birkie ca'd a lord . . .') and he was moved to anger, and to satirical verse, by an incident at Inveraray during a tour of the Highlands. He couldn't get attention at the inn because the innkeeper and all the staff were busy with the demands of an aristocratic party, visitors bound for the Castle. He scratched verses on a window-pane, sometimes read as a slight on Inveraray, but really full of a hungry traveller's resentment. It wasn't exactly the innkeeper's fault. Let's blame the feudal system. Let's make it personal and blame His Grace the Duke of Argyll:

Whoe'er he be that sojourns here,
I pity much his case,
Unless he come to wait upon
The Lord their God, his Grace.

There's naething here but Highland pride,
And Highland scab and hunger;
If Providence has sent me here,
'Twas surely in an anger.

So there has been outward respect and hidden anger, paternalism in a good and a very bad sense: between the big house and the tenantry, the rest of Scotland, there can hardly be an easy relationship. There's too much history, too much baggage. Naomi Mitchison, a laird by birth but not by inclination, expresses it in simple terms in her children's novel *The Big House*:

He knew, and she knew, and each knew that the other knew, the reason why
they had set on her. That was because she was from the Big House, and in times
past the Big House ones had been hard and cruel to the fathers and grandfathers
of the ones at the school, and kept them in fear and, maybe, put them out of their
houses, but now the thing had turned round and they had revenged themselves.
And it was all as senseless as could be, but there is the way things are.

Mitchison struggled with the problem in her own life, and her diaries show that she tried very hard to be a good laird in Carradale, the estate in Kintyre where she lived for over sixty years. But to her distress, at one point, she came across a rumour that the local people were taking a different, and very West Highland, view:

> . . . saying why on earth was I playing at farming . . . it may be at least half true,
> and if it is, then everyone is laughing at me, even my own men. I felt like chucking
> the whole thing, but yet I couldn't. I've taken on commitments of various kinds.

That's probably the worst, the killer realisation, as you sit in the big house. You have plenty of commitments, plenty of problems, possibly as many as your tenants have, though of a different sort. You're doing your best, for the estate, for them. What thanks do you get? They laugh at you. They don't like you. They can't even be bothered to hate you. They just think you're irrelevant, or a nuisance, like J. J. Haldane Burgess in Shetland viewing the gentry as 'da dokkin on da scroo', the dockweed on the cornstack:

> Dir usliss deevils here an dere
> Ipo Gud's frutfil laand,
> At for da pur hae deil-a-care,
> Dey muv no fit or haand.
> Bit Laabir, feth! will conquer yit
> In spite o aa, I view.
> Dir aristocracies is bit
> Da dokkin on da scroo.

But there's the big house, part of the landscape of Scotland. Around it stretches the real Scotland. Can they ever meet? In William Soutar's poetic vision, they do:

> There's a puckle lairds in the auld house
> wha haud the waas thegither:
> there's no muckle graith in the auld house
> nor smeddum aither . . .
>
> Let's caa in the folk to the auld house
> the puir folk aa thegither:
> it's sunkit on rock is the auld house,
> and the rock's their brither.

It was aince a braw and bauld house
and guid for onie weather:
but the folk maun funder the auld house
and bigg up anither.

The two images come together. The old house, the castle or the mansion, part of Scotland, is brought out of its aristocratic seclusion, shaken clear of its trappings of authority, to gather the people together and stand for Scotland itself.

10 Small Town Blues

At night we came to Banff,
where I remember nothing that particularly
claimed my attention.

Dr Samuel Johnson

Small towns and villages: where would Scottish literature be without them? In earliest times the landscape was one of scattered cottages and 'ferm touns'. Here and there a toun – the grouping of bothies, barns and byres round a farm steading – became important locally. Sometimes it gained this position because it was the nearest settlement to the castle, the mill or the parish church – placenames containing the words Milton or Kirkton, for instance, are clues to that – and so was the logical site for a market or fair. Obviously it was also the best place to open an alehouse. George Mackay Brown addresses the first innkeepers in Hamnavoe, which developed into the Orkney town of Stromness:

> You did not live to see
> On the steep dyked westward park
> The merchants' houses rising,
> William and Mareon Clark;
>
> Tall houses hewn from granite,
> Piers on the tidal mark,
> Yawl and cobble noust-gathered,
> William and Mareon Clark . . .

So we began to get the towns which (even if Banff, on the peaceful coast of the Moray Firth, did not inspire Dr Johnson to any memorable observation) have made their impression, for better or worse, on the minds of Scottish writers. It was Lord Cockburn in the early nineteenth century – not only a judge but a writer of journals and memoirs – who is said to have coined the phrase 'As quiet as the grave – or Peebles'. Edwin Muir, on the other hand, touring Scotland in the years between the two World Wars, found the little towns of the Borders to have a 'curiously wakeful and vivid air'. He called it curious, he explained, because:

> . . . most of the other small towns I have seen in Scotland are contentedly or
> morosely lethargic, sunk in a fatalistic dullness broken only by scandalmongering
> and such alarums as drinking produces; a dead silence punctuated by malicious
> whispers and hiccups.

Jane Welsh, later the wife of Thomas Carlyle and a letter-writer of genius, had similar reservations about her East Lothian home town of Haddington when she was a lively young woman still living with her mother:

Here I am once more at the bottom of this pit of dullness, hemmed in all round . . .
It is the dimmest, dullest spot (I verily believe) in the Creator's universe: to look
round in it, one might imagine that time had made a stand: the shopkeepers are
to be seen standing at the doors of their shops, in the very same posture in which
they have stood there ever since I was born.

It's fair to acknowledge that some writers, on the other hand, are fond of the small-town atmosphere, lulled to tranquillity by the very fact that, as Jane Welsh observed, 'the thing that hath been is that also which shall be'. Jane herself remembered her childhood days with affection, just as Hugh MacDiarmid recalled Langholm in Dumfriesshire and his happy boyhood there:

Nae maitter hoo faur I've travelled sinsyne
The cast o' Dumfriesshire's aye in me like wine;
And my sangs are gleids o' the candent spirit
    Its sons inherit.

And the Argyll novelist Neil Munro assured the townspeople of his birthplace, 'I never could keep Inveraray out of any story of mine and I never will.' The unnamed 'burgh town' of his novel *The Daft Days* is unmistakably the Inveraray of his nineteenth-century childhood, remembered with love:

The town's bell rang through the dark of the winter morning with queer little jolts
and pauses, as if Wanton Wully Oliver, the ringer, had been jovial the night before.
A blithe New-Year-time bell; a droll, daft, scatter-brained bell . . . The burgh town
turned on its pillows, drew up its feet from the bed-bottles, last night hot, now
turned to chilly stone, rubbed its eyes, and knew by that bell it was the daftest
of the daft days come.

Looking back on the small town and its life as they used to be – that's a favourite view. John Galt's *Annals of the Parish* was published in 1821, but he is concerned to show the development from clachan to town of his Ayrshire community between 1760 and 1810. Early in his chronicle the building of a new road 'turns the town inside out':

It was agreed among the heritors that it should run along the back-side of the
south houses; and that there should be steadings fewed off on each side, according
to a plan that was laid down, and this being gone into, the town gradually, in the
course of years, grew up into that orderliness which makes it now a pattern to the
country-side . . .

J. M. Barrie's Thrums is definitely Kirriemuir, where he was born, but it's the Kirriemuir of his mother's time, the early nineteenth century, not his own. Handloom weaving was then the main occupation in a thriving, yet still rural, Kirriemuir. About 1870, when Barrie was ten years old, the old cottage industry was overtaken by new methods based on power looms, and changes came to the town: dams, chimney-stacks, demolished houses, the roar of machinery. Barrie dwells lovingly on 'the thing that hath been':

> Thrums is the name I give here to a handful of houses jumbled together in a cup,
> which is the town nearest the schoolhouse . . . The road that climbs from the
> square, which is Thrums' heart, to the north is so steep and straight that in
> a sharp frost children hunker at the top and are blown down with a roar and a
> rush on rails of ice. At such times, when viewed from the cemetery where the
> traveller from the schoolhouse gets his first glimpse of the little town, Thrums
> is but two church steeples and a dozen red patches standing out of a snow heap.

Violet Jacob, Barrie's near contemporary and also born in Angus, also praises 'the braw, braw toon o' Kirrie' in one of her poems. However, her praise, and the way in which she expresses it, has a different, ironic intention:

> There's an auld wife bides in Kirrie – set her up! a pridefu' cratur –
> And she's crackin' aye o' London an' the grand fowk ye may see;
> O' the king, an' syne his palace, till I'm sure I'm like to hate her,
> For the mairket-day in Kirrie is the sicht for me.
> But ye ken I'm sweir to fash her, an' it's best to be agreein',
> For gin ye dinna heed her, then she's cankered-like an' soor,
> Dod, she tells o' muckle lairnin' – but I doot the bizzar's leein',
> For it's fules wad bide in London when they kent o' Kirriemuir.

The speaker of these lines thinks there's no place like Kirrie. She is perfectly happy in her own wee town. There's nothing wrong with it, except of course that stuck-up besom who keeps going on about other places far away. This (as Jacob knows very well) is the voice of the kailyard, or cabbage-patch, a view of life which tended to hinder the development of Scottish fiction about the end of the nineteenth century, and which can be seen in some popular writing even today.

Barrie with his Thrums sketches and Ian Maclaren with such novels as *Beside the Bonnie Brier Bush* are among the leading lights of the 'kailyard school'. (Its name comes from a line by Burns – 'There grows a bonnie brier bush in oor kailyard' – from which Maclaren took his title.) The characters, in general, live in small towns,

cultivating their own kailyards and disapproving, or suspicious, of anyone new or different. They order their lives according to the rule of the Kirk and the wise old dominie. There's a lot of death and suffering, but it is stoically borne. They are hedged in by barriers of strict morality and convention, and they don't want to break out. Why should they, when all is for the best?

Unfortunately, life is not always so tidy, and Scottish writers were alert enough to see the flaw in the kailyard idyll. The backlash, a bitter one, came in 1901 with George Douglas Brown's novel *The House with the Green Shutters*. His small town of Barbie is the right sort of place for kailyard goings-on, but, as well as being steeped in death and disaster, it is a frankly-depicted nest of gossip and malice. The 'bodies', village worthies, comment in a sneering chorus on anyone seen to be doing better than themselves, with particular attention to John Gourlay the carrier and what they see as his undeserved wealth:

> They were standing at the Cross, to enjoy their Saturday at e'en, when Gourlay's 'quarriers' – as the quarry horses had been named – came through the town last week-end. There were groups of bodies in the streets, washed from toil to enjoy the quiet air; dandering slowly or gossiping at ease; and they all turned to watch the quarriers stepping bravely up, their heads tossing to the hill. The big-men-in-a-small-way glowered and said nothing.
>
> 'I wouldn't mind,' said Sandy Toddle at last, 'I wouldn't mind if he weren't such a demned ess!'

Possibly Barbie is as exaggerated in one direction as Drumtochty and Thrums are in the other, but after *The House with the Green Shutters* it was difficult to look at small towns and villages in quite the same way again, or to write about them kailyard-fashion without irony. Lorna Moon, brought up in the north-east village of Strichen at the end of the nineteenth century, emigrated to America and, from there, before her early death, published two books set in her home district. They weren't well received in Strichen. Her spare, realistic stories occasionally slip in the direction of melodrama, but in 'The Corp' she is in control and making merciless fun of kailyard customs. Old Kirsty Fraser is worried that she may not be allowed to view the corpse of Sandy MacNab, who has choked on a cold potato:

And who in all Drumorty would think of being buried without Kirsty Fraser to cry
as the lid was screwed down? Had she no' cried at every funeral for forty-five years?
And was it no' part and parcel of the ceremony for her to have a fit when the body
was carried out? And was it no' true that the laddies of the village hung round the
house of sorrow waiting for the chance to run for the doctor to bring her round?

Village gossip was something Naomi Mitchison knew all about. Coming from a bohemian London life to
settle in Carradale, she considered and explored the reasons why village life might be less than idyllic:

Life is dull. There is little alternative employment for young men; those who are
ambitious . . . go to the towns, where they are not necessarily happy. Whereas
dullness drives young people away, it drives some of the older ones to drink.
And it drives the girls and women into endless, pointless gossip and quarrelling,
family feuds, church feuds, feuds between the 'Rural' and the Gaelic Choir,
one vast series of mole-hills talked into mountains!

In her novel *Lobsters on the Agenda* she turns this into fiction, following the events of one week in a Highland
village. No melodrama here: the choir and the village hall committee are fitted in between church services and
meeting the twice-weekly steamer. A mystery keeps the talk going: who stole the lobsters? A hint of old magic:
was it an ill-wishing spell that caused the unpleasant teacher to catch the measles? The people of the village
rub along together, though not always in kailyard bliss. The character Kate Snow, an 'incomer' like Mitchison,
has her own thoughts on the matter:

You could sum up the Highland way of life, she thought, if you were unkind,
in four words: devilment, obligement, refreshment, buggerment.

After a spell of city novels, small towns have recently come back into the literary frame in Scotland. Alan Warner
does something new and exciting by taking the sedate tourist centre of Oban – gateway to the romantic West
Highlands, a prime case for Kailyard treatment – and showing us, instead, a town full of angst and unemploy-
ment, oddness and spirit. The central character in his novel *Morvern Callar* finds her lover dead on the floor,
and after some consideration cuts his body into pieces and distributes the parcels among the heathery hills.
The schoolgirls in *The Sopranos* make the long journey to a singing contest in Edinburgh with every intention
of flunking out, in order to allow more time for exploring the city's clubs and bars. They're not going to be
caged and circumscribed by living in a small town. They see what Alan Warner sees:

> . . . a town hunched round a harbour like a classical amphitheatre, where the
> ocean grew still in a trapped bay an the mountains of the islands seemed to hang
> in the skies of summer nights . . . where clouds would always move faster than
> anywhere these girls would ever travel to and where the dying light of day would
> falter in the slow-moving coal-fire smoke above where owls an foxes moved in
> the grey-black woods of the shelterin hills, hundreds of feet above the bus-stops.

They know what Jane Welsh knows and what the kailyard novelists tend to forget: the small town, the village and the people who live there are elements in an infinitely wide world.

11 Shrieking Steam

An' the flame-tappit furnaces staun' in a raw,
A' bleezin', an' blawin', an' smeekin' awa,
Their eerie licht brichtenin' the laigh hingin' cluds
Gleamin' far ower the loch an' the mirk lanely wuds.

Janet Hamilton

In 1765 the engineer James Watt, strolling on Glasgow Green, had a brainwave. 'I had gone as far as the Herd's house,' he said later, 'when the idea came into my mind, that as steam was an elastic body it would rush into a vacuum . . .' A far-reaching sequence of events was sparked off at that moment. We tend to call it the Industrial Revolution.

The new industries – and the old ones, for there had been mining in the Leadhills area of Lanarkshire since at least the thirteenth century – could not have existed without the resources of the land. Leadhills was known as 'God's treasure-house in Scotland' with its yield of lead, gold, and the silver which could be refined from lead ore. Allan Ramsay, who moved to Edinburgh at the beginning of the eighteenth century to become a wigmaker, bookseller, anthologist and poet, was proud to recall that he had been born the son of a mine manager there:

> Of *Crawford-Moor*, born in *Leadhill*,
> Where Min'ral Springs *Glengonnar* fill,
> Which joins sweet flowing *Clyde* . . .

But these industries changed the landscape radically and for ever. Even today bare hillsides at Wanlockhead, near Leadhills, show the effect of the lead fumes which killed off all vegetation. The first mills used water-power, and their buildings appeared on the banks of fast-flowing streams like the Tay and Ericht in Perthshire and the Levern and Black Cart in Renfrewshire. Not only the rural scenery was affected, but the way of life, as John Galt's narrator records in *Annals of the Parish*:

> It had been often remarked by ingenious men, that the Brawl burn, which ran
> through the parish, though a small, was yet a rapid stream, and had a wonderful
> capacity for damming, and to turn mills . . . A proposal came from Glasgow to
> build a cotton-mill on its banks, beneath the Witch-linn . . . A spacious fabric it
> was – nothing like it had been seen before in our day and generation – and, for the
> people that were brought to work in it, a new town was built in the vicinity . . .

As steam power – James Watt's idea – took over, it became necessary to build factories near coalfields, or by canals which could transport coal to them. The 'heavy industries' of textile manufacture, coal-mining, shipbuilding and engineering covered great tracts of the countryside with buildings and equipment, and brought people from rural areas to live where the work was. Some of Scotland prospered; some of Scotland declined.

All of this was observed by writers, who responded in different ways. Some were excited by the new possibilities, like the 'canal poets' of the central belt who sang the wonders of the Forth and Clyde Canal, completed at the end of the eighteenth century (and now being restored and re-opened for traffic). William Muir could see that one barge had the power of half-a-dozen horses:

> Wi' something that the learn'd ca' *steam*,
> That drives at heugh the wa'king-beam
> O' huge engines, to drain coal seam,
> > Or carry hutches,
> She in her breast swells sic a faem,
> > As has few matches.

Some were just stimulated by the new sights and sounds in their world, like John Davidson in 'this grey town' – his home town of Greenock in Renfrewshire, suddenly a busy port and centre of shipbuilding and sugar manufacture – which 'pipes the morning up before the lark', he wrote, 'with shrieking steam', or James Macfarlan finding a wild beauty in industrial Glasgow:

> Mighty furnaces are flaring like a demon's breath of fire,
> Forges, like great burning cities, break in many a crimson spire;
> Tongues of eager flame are lapping all the glory of the heaven,
> While a blush of burning hectic o'er the midnight's face is driven.

Some poets are less ready to proclaim that new means better. Thomas Campbell, who found fame far from his birthplace of Glasgow, complains on a visit home about a sad difference in the river Clyde. Instead of a 'daisied green-sward' along its banks, he objects, 'unsightly brick-lanes smoke, and clanking engines gleam.' And Janet Hamilton, who spent her long life in the weaving village of Langloan, now part of Coatbridge in Lanarkshire, loved as a young woman to stroll to the attractively-named Summerlee. Latterly it wasn't such a pleasant walk:

> Oot-owre the auld brig, up to sweet Simmerlee,
> Sweet, said ye? – hech, whaur? – for nae sweetness I see;
> Big lums spewin' reek an' red lowe on the air,
> Steam snorin' an' squallin', and whiles muckle mair!
>
> Explodin' an' smashin' an' crashin', an' then
> The wailin' o' women an' groanin' o' men,
> A' scowther't an' mangle't, sae painfu' to see –
> The sweetness is gane, noo it's black Simmerlee.

Nevertheless Janet Hamilton wrote of her hope that industry, properly organised, would improve the lot of the working classes, which from her own experience she knew had been far from idyllic in the old days. All too often, however, the hard work, the overcrowded houses, the meagre pay made things much worse. Throughout the nineteenth century and beyond there was an undercurrent of angry expression about working conditions and social evils. Sometimes the poetry and prose attained only local publication, like much of the material in Tom Leonard's anthology *Radical Renfrew* which at last, in 1990, brought this strand of Scottish writing back into the light. Sometimes in its unaffected realism it did attract attention, like Patrick MacGill's semi-autobiographical novels *Children of the Dead End* and *The Rat-Pit*, about the plight of Irish immigrant workers:

> I got a job on the railway and obtained lodgings in a dismal and crooked street,
> which was a den of disfigured children and a hothouse of precocious passion, in
> the south side of Glasgow . . . We slept in the one room, mother, children and
> myself, and all through the night the children yelled like cats in the moonshine.

Mary Brooksbank knew what it was like in the jute mills of Dundee, where 'they fairly mak' ye work for your ten-an'-nine', while Ellen Johnston, also a factory worker, expressed the universal sentiment tersely: 'What care some gentry if they're weel though a' the puir wad dee?' Joe Corrie, a miner who finally managed to leave the pits and gain freedom to write poems and plays, says it all in a few lines:

> Crawlin' about like a snail in the mud,
> Covered wi' clammy blae,
> ME, made after the image o' God –
> Jings! but it's laughable, tae.

A generation later, when the car factory in Linwood opened with considerable fanfare (turning a rural Renfrewshire village into a town overnight), Jeff Torrington found things hadn't changed much. 'The Widow' is the main assembly line:

> Yeah, tighten that bolt, bud!
> Drive that screw!
> You won't escape The Widow
> Till she's had'r due:
> That mean ol bitch
> Ain't gonna grant you no spell
> Till she's worked you to the bone
> On the Devil's Carousel.

And William McIlvanney, who had dealt with the Ayrshire miners of his grandfather's generation in his novel *Docherty*, returned to the subject – and the effect – of manual labour in *The Kiln*. Young Tam takes a holiday job in the brickwork, wondering whether to stay there or go to university, the first of his family to have such a choice. Certainly he hates the brickwork, where he discovers that time is 'divided into one-hour units':

> For an hour you sit at the machine and pick up the unbaked black bricks that spew out at you relentlessly and stack them on a hutch . . . For an hour, while someone else becomes an extension of the machine, you push the loaded hutches out of the lighted shed into the darkness and along the rails that lead to the kiln. One of the two men in the kiln accepts the full hutch and you bring the empty one back to the shed to be reloaded. For an hour you sweep the shed and try to remember that you're not a robot. Then you return to unloading the bricks.

What Tam doesn't see at that stage, but McIlvanney with hindsight does, is something else about the uncongenial work, its strangeness, its pecking order, its threats. In the novel it is the works bully who expresses it: 'The kiln is where cley either hardens intae brick or breaks down intae rubbish.' In the story of a man's life the brickwork scenes are only one element, but the title of the novel has been chosen with care.

Over time the industrial landscape can come to be accepted, almost unnoticed, in its pervasive presence. The beat novelist Alexander Trocchi, brought up in Glasgow, finds a harsh beauty on the Forth and Clyde Canal:

> Up on deck the air was cool, cool grey, and over behind the sheds the brick factory-stack was enveloped in a stagnant mushroom of its own yellow smoke . . . The water was smooth and scum-laden and it seemed to lean against us and fall again, the surface broken with scum-spittles, as we made way . . . Soon we were chugging along the banks of the canal and it rolled along behind us like a very neat black tape dividing two masses of green-brown countryside.

And there's poetry to be found in the very work, as Colin Donati celebrates the centenary of the building of the great landmark rail bridge across the Forth:

> knitting and riveting
> pinning and weaving
> knitting and riveting
> pinning and weaving
> building the girders out
> over the water

> gangers and riveters
> sweating at furnaces
> welding the rivet-tongs
> hammering plates in place
> hanging the arms
> of the great cantilever . . .

But what we have today is best called a post-industrial landscape. That was prefigured in George Blake's novel *The Shipbuilders* as early as the depression-hit 1930s, when a shipyard owner sails down the once-bustling river Clyde:

> Yard after yard passed by, the berths empty, the grass growing about the sinking keel-blocks . . . A tradition, a skill, a glory, a passion, was visibly in decay and all the acquired and inherited loveliness of artistry rotting along the banks of the stream.

Blake's phrase is 'the high, tragic pageant of the Clyde'. Edwin Morgan has captured the river's present-day malaise in a few more perfect words: 'The great sick Clyde shivers in its bed'. But the altered landscape is not just on the Clyde, of course, and the trouble is not just in shipbuilding. Throughout the industrial central belt of Scotland, traditional occupations like engineering have been seen to give way to 'sunrise industries' which, in their turn, sometimes, see the sun go down. Beside the M8 motorway which joins Glasgow and Edinburgh, the pit bings that dot the countryside like the mountains of the moon – heaps of spoil from coalmining days – are being 'landscaped' – it's a current term – and grassed over, while a series of massive artworks symbolise past industrial glories.

Edwin Morgan's visionary poem sequence *Sonnets from Scotland* brings us up to date and beyond. His space-travellers find in a bog an old pound coin belonging to a Scottish republic, which in real life has not yet come about. As in so many of his poems, we are reminded that you never know what may happen. Post-industrial doesn't mean finished:

> The marshy scurf crept up to our machine,
> sucked at our boots. Yet nothing seemed ill-starred.
> And least of all the realm the coin contained.

12 Cityscape

I saw rain falling and the rainbow drawn
On Lammermuir. Hearkening I heard again
In my precipitous city beaten bells
Winnow the keen sea wind . . .

R. L. Stevenson

At the time this book was being written there were only four recognised cities in Scotland, though Inverness was awarded city status in 2000. Historically a town might become a city for various reasons of church or state, so that Perth is known as 'the Fair City' and there's a football team called Brechin City. Lewis Grassic Gibbon personified the four official cities in the 1930s. Edinburgh he characterised as 'a disappointed spinster with a hare-lip and inhibitions', Dundee as 'a frowsy fisher-wife addicted to gin and infanticide', Aberdeen as 'a thin-lipped peasant woman who has borne eleven and buried nine'. Then there was Glasgow, which Gibbon couldn't quite find words for. He tried 'the vomit of a cataleptic commercialism', but decided that wasn't quite right. 'It may be a corpse,' was his next suggestion, 'but the maggot-swarm upon it is very fiercely alive'.

And in some moods other Scottish writers have seen only the bad side of city life. Lord Cockburn in the mid-nineteenth century considered Dundee 'the palace of Scottish blackguardism, unless perhaps Paisley be entitled to contest this honour with it'. Hugh MacDiarmid particularly disliked Glasgow, where he lived for a short but uncongenial time:

Where have I seen a human being looking
As Glasgow looked this gin-clear evening – with face and fingers
A cadaverous blue, hand-clasp slimy and cold
As that of a corpse, finger-nails grown immeasurably long,
As they do in the grave, little white eyes, and hardly
Any face at all?

Edwin Muir also hated Glasgow. His family moved there from Orkney when he was fourteen, and culture-shock, together with family tragedy, made Glasgow for him a nightmare place:

. . . if I was tired or ill I often had the feeling, passing through Eglinton Street
or Crown Street, that I was dangerously close to the ground, deep down in a place
from which I might never be able to climb up again . . . the slums seemed to be
everywhere around me, a great, spreading swamp into which I might sink for good.

Visitors have always loved Edinburgh, but at one time the Old Town sanitary arrangements were apt to come as a shock to the unsuspecting, and Tobias Smollett in the eighteenth century couldn't resist letting a character in his novel *Humphry Clinker* comment on them. ('Gardy-loo' is thought to be a corruption of a French phrase with a literal meaning of 'beware of the water', but Win Jenkins's rather free translation certainly gets to the point.)

> Behold there is nurro jakes [lavatory] in the whole kingdom, nor anything for
> poor sarvants, but a barrel with tongs thrown across; and all the chairs [commodes]
> in the family are emptied into this here barrel once a day; and at ten o'clock at
> night the whole cargo is flung out of a back window that looks into some street
> or lane, and the maid calls 'gardy loo' to the passengers which signifies 'Lord have
> mercy on you!'

But of course that isn't the whole story. Scotland's cities have found poets to praise them ever since William Dunbar, in the fifteenth century, wrote 'Blyth Aberdeen, thou beryl of all towns . . .' Aberdeen is rather proud to claim a connection with the bad Lord Byron – there's a statue outside the Grammar School which he attended – whose mother's family were landed gentry on Deeside. There's even a legend that Shakespeare came to Aberdeen with the actors' company which played there in 1601. Where else would he have learned about a blasted heath near Forres?

Perhaps the essential statement about Aberdeen – its grey glittering streets, its strong people, the sea essential to this harbour town – is Alexander Scott's long poem 'Heart of Stone':

> . . . And hirplan hame half-drouned wi the weicht o herrin
> The trauchled trawler waffs in her wake
> A flaffer o wings – a flash o faem-white feathers –
> As the sea-maw spires i the stane-gray lift
> Owre sworlan swaws o the stane-gray sea
> And sclents til the sea-gray toun, the hert o stane.

But there's much more, and the ancient university can show many literary graduates who have written about their alma mater. These include Gaelic poets, like Iain Crichton Smith and Derick Thomson, because Aberdeen was for generations, geographically, the most accessible university for the islands. Writing his poem sequence 'A Life' years later, Crichton Smith devoted eight poems to 'Aberdeen University 1945–1949', a time of discovery:

> Aberdeen, I constantly evoke
> your geometry of roses.
>
> Your beads of salt
> decorate my wrists

and are the tiny bells
of grammar schools.

There are no deaths
that I recall

among your cinemas,
in the shadows

of your green trees.
Aberdeen,

I loved your granite
your salt mica.

Your light
taught
me immortality.

That mica, which makes the granite buildings of Aberdeen sparkle in the clear North Sea air, turns up, too, in a poem by G. S. Fraser: 'Glitter of mica at the windy corners . . .' The Aberdeenshire writer Jessie Kesson chose *Glitter of Mica* as the title of her second novel. Kesson longed to go to university, but she was brought up in an orphanage during the 1920s and 1930s and that ambition was seen by the Trustees as ludicrously unsuitable for a child in her position, particularly a girl. The frustration remained:

O the regret as a body growes auld!
I wad hae likit a scarlet goon
an' a desk o' my ain 'neath the auld, grey Croon . . .

In 1987, by then recognised as an important writer, Kesson was invited to receive an honorary degree at Aberdeen, and got her scarlet goon at last.

The end of the twentieth century has brought great changes to Aberdeen, some at least due to the discovery of North Sea oil. Ian Rankin's policeman Inspector Rebus, pursuing a suspect north to Aberdeen and Shetland, finds plenty of information in his hotel room:

Since the early seventies, the area's population had increased by sixty thousand . . .
major new suburbs . . . the world's busiest heliport . . . [and] the minor mention
of a fishing village called Old Torry, which had been granted its charter three years
after Columbus landed in America. When oil came to the north-east, Old Torry was
flattened to make way for a Shell supply base. Rebus raised his glass and toasted the
memory of the village.

Yet something particular to Aberdeen remains: a tenacity, a granite quality perhaps? The central character in
Leila Aboulela's *The Translator*, a young Sudanese woman working in Aberdeen, sees this when an unusually
heavy snowfall brings traffic to a halt:

Chaos was a rare visitor to this orderly city. It was flustered now, tense and
stubborn as it insisted on following its daily rhythm. Shops must open, people
must get to work. That was sacred. If Sammar had searched for anything sacred
to this city and not found it, here it was.

Though Dundee, like Aberdeen, is an old and distinguished town, its history as a city has been an interrupted
one, and in 1888 it applied for the title in the modern, official sense. The poet James Young Geddes felt that
the town was denying its stirring, radical history by wanting to be a city, and shouldn't be rejoicing quite so
extravagantly when it succeeded. 'Shall we now,' he enquired, 'claim precedence of Liverpool, Glasgow, Perth
(especially Perth)?'

Perth will be brought low;
Perth will be no longer cock of the walk;
Perth may no longer claim pre-eminence in the river;
Her Lord Provost shall no longer be Admiral of the Tay.
We will bite our thumbs at Perth;
We will chuck out our tongues to her –
So shall our souls be satisfied.

The literary history of Dundee includes its privilege of nurturing the poetic talent of William McGonagall.
He wrote later of the day he discovered he was a poet, describing it as the most startling incident of his life.

A flame, as Lord Byron has said, seemed to kindle up my entire frame, along with a strong desire to write poetry; and I felt so happy, so happy, that I was inclined to dance . . . I imagined that a pen was in my right hand, and a voice crying 'Write! Write!'

His muse ranged widely in space and time, but McGonagall never failed to praise Dundee and to chronicle events of local interest, such as the Tay Bridge disaster on (as his poem specifies) 'the last Sabbath day of 1879':

As soon as the catastrophe came to be known
The alarm from mouth to mouth was blown,
And the cry rang out all o'er the town,
Good Heavens! the Tay Bridge is blown down . . .

But there's a lot more to Dundee than McGonagall, as poets like John Burnside, Don Paterson and W. N. Herbert are proving today. Herbert uses in some of his poetry the unique accent, or voice, of Dundee:

Well Eh luked up at grey gulls skriekan
Eh luked doon at peopul speakan
and Eh swerr there wiz nae difference in thi soond
as Eh daunnert thru thi streets
lissnin til thi girns and greets
o thi sowels that flew an waulked thru Dundee Toun.

When we come to Edinburgh, it's all been said, and by the most prestigious names. Scott is only one of those who have found a good phrase for the old city:

Such dusky grandeur cloth'd the height,
Where the huge Castle holds its state,
And all the steep slope down,
Whose ridgy back heaves to the sky,
Pil'd deep and massy, close and high,
Mine own romantic town!

The truly extraordinary thing is the way that poets have left their mark on Edinburgh. It's not just a question of monuments and statues: unexpected treats lie in store, like looking from the Allan Ramsay statue in Princes Street towards the colourful gables of Ramsay Garden and realising that the complex of buildings still contains, somewhere within, the octagonal shape of the Goose Pie House which the poet built in 1733.

Four poets are evoked by one slightly dishevelled grave in Canongate kirkyard, along the Royal Mile. The tall grey tombstone bears a verse in eighteenth-century script:

> No sculptured Marble here, nor pompous lay,
> No storied Urn nor animated Bust:
> This simple Stone directs pale Scotia's way
> To pour her Sorrows o'er her Poet's Dust.

The lines are by Burns, and this is the grave of Robert Fergusson, the most Edinburgh of poets, a lively young eighteenth-century man-about-town, the poet of all the city's dirt and beauty: 'Auld Reekie! wale o' ilka town that Scotland kens beneath the moon . . .' Burns greatly admired Fergusson, but the two poets never met. When Burns came to Edinburgh in 1787, to be for a time the toast of the literati and the ardent friend of the lady he called Clarinda, Fergusson was already dead and buried in a pauper's grave. 'O thou, my elder brother in misfortune,' Burns wrote, shocked at such a fate, 'by far my elder brother in the Muse . . .' He paid for a headstone for 'poor Fergusson', and – a far greater gift – wrote his epitaph.

A hundred years later Robert Louis Stevenson also admired Fergusson, feeling a strong affinity with him:

> I had always a great sense of kinship with poor Robert Fergusson – so clever
> a boy, so wild, of such a mixed strain, so unfortunate, born in the same town
> with me, and, as I always felt, rather by express intimation than from evidence,
> so like myself.

He planned to have the stone repaired and re-dedicated, 'as the gift of one Edinburgh lad to another', but died in Samoa before it could be arranged. In 1962, when the Saltire Society finally carried out the repairs, Robert Garioch, another Edinburgh poet who felt strangely close to Fergusson, attended the rededication ceremony. The sonnet he wrote on that chilly October day draws all the ghosts together.

Canongait kirkyaird in the failing year
is auld and grey, the wee roseirs are bare;
five gulls leam white agin the dirty air:
why are they here? There's naething for them here.

Why are we here oursels? We gaither near
the grave. Fergusons mainly, quite a fair
turn-out, respectfu, ill at ease, we stare
at daith – there's an address – I canna hear.

Aweill, we staund bareheidit in the haar,
murnin a man that gaed back til the pool
twa-hunner year afore our time. The glaur

that haps his banes glowres back. Strang, present dool
ruggs at my hairt. Lichtlie this gin ye daur:
here Robert Burns knelt and kissed the mool.

Stevenson wrote lovingly about his city – even though he considered that it had 'one of the vilest climates under heaven', with the wind, rain, fog and snow that hardly suited his delicate health – and his psychological masterpiece *The Strange Case of Dr Jekyll and Mr Hyde* is set in a London which everybody recognises as very like Edinburgh. 'Man is not truly one, but truly two,' discovers Henry Jekyll, and many writers have noted the same duality in Edinburgh: New Town and Old Town, wealth and poverty, respectability and vice. The city can change its aspect in a moment, as Muriel Spark notes:

It was then that Miss Brodie looked beautiful and fragile, just as dark, heavy
Edinburgh itself could suddenly be changed into a floating city when the light was
a special pearly white and fell upon one of the gracefully fashioned streets.

Garioch was one of the poets immortalised in Alexander Moffat's 1980 painting 'Poets' Pub'. There they are in an imaginary howff, meant to recall Rose Street pubs like Milne's Bar or the Abbotsford where the literati gathered during the 1950s and 1960s: Edinburgh residents like Garioch, Norman MacCaig and Sydney Goodsir Smith, together with friends from other corners of Scotland like Hugh MacDiarmid, George Mackay Brown, Edwin Morgan, Sorley MacLean and Iain Crichton Smith. It was a remarkable generation of poets, coinciding too with the early years of the Edinburgh International Festival. Garioch didn't fail to commemorate

the way the Festival turns the old city into something rich and strange: 'In simmer, whan aa sorts foregether,' he wrote, 'in Embro to the ploy.'

Robert Fergusson as a poet would have enjoyed the International Festival, but as a drinker and clubber he would also have understood Irvine Welsh's novel *Trainspotting*. This is Edinburgh life too. The character Renton muses on a day which has included an episode with opium suppositories:

> At the bus stop, ah realised what a sweltering hot day it had become.
> Ah remembered somebody sais that it wis the first day ay the Festival.
> Well, they certainly got the weather fir it. Ah sat oan the wall by the bus stop,
> letting the sun soak intae ma wet jeans. Ah saw a 32 coming, but didnae move,
> through apathy. The next one that came, ah got it thegither tae board the fucker
> and headed back tae Sunny Leith. It really is time tae clean up, ah thought,
> as ah mounted the stairs ay ma new flat.

And Fergusson, Renton and the Rose Street poets would all find something to recognise in Ian Rankin's Edinburgh. It's sometimes said that Rankin's crime novels are set in the underworld of Edinburgh, but in fact they are more subtle than that. They show tourist Edinburgh, official Edinburgh, the city you see around you, and then turn it over to show the unsuspected underside: duality again.

The result is that you walk through Parliament Square on a sunny day in the middle of the Festival and picture a real body on a scaffold, as in Rankin's short story 'A Good Hanging'. You pass the entrance to Mary King's Close and wonder if there's someone strung up to one of the ceiling hooks down there, as in *Mortal Causes*. You pass the Scottish Parliament and recall that Rankin has embarked on a trilogy about that enterprise, starting with *Set in Darkness*. Rankin's Edinburgh is at one and the same time the city you see and a landscape on its own.

While Edinburgh is readily seen as a poetic sort of place, it's perhaps more surprising to find a wealth of poetry (and fiction, and drama) in the more industrial, less obviously romantic city of Glasgow. But Glasgow grew so quickly that poets found a certain exhilaration in its noise and bustle, its very difference from the countryside. Alexander Smith evokes this strange wild beauty:

Draw thy fierce streams of blinding ore,
Smite on a thousand anvils, roar
      Down to the harbour-bars;
Smoulder in smoky sunsets, flare
On rainy nights, with street and square
      Lie empty to the stars.
From terrace proud to alley base
I know thee as my mother's face.

Famously, too, Glasgow is a many-sided city, and every aspect has appeared in its literature. The dirty old industrial Glasgow which had grown up almost haphazardly over the years was celebrated by poets like John Kincaid:

Eh, ma citie o raucle sang,
ma braid stane citie wi dwaums o steel.
Eh, ma Glesca, ma mither o revolt,
dauran the wunds o time in a raggit shawl.
Eh ma hanselt hinnie wi scaurs o war,
ma twalmonth lassock, ma carlin ages auld.

But the prosperous middle-class families in Guy McCrone's novel *Wax Fruit* live comfortably in the West End:

A Victorian row, 'commanding a beautiful view of the brilliant parterres of the
Botanic Gardens, with the umbrageous woods of Kelvinside beyond', set back from
the placid, easy-going traffic of a Great Western Road where once in a while a green
car rattled past on its way to and from Kirklee . . .

There was, as there still is, the West End Park at Kelvingrove, 'with its beautiful flowers and trees so green', to quote McGonagall, but also the people's park of Glasgow Green, with its long history, both good and bad, as Ian Hamilton senses:

Deep in its rut the river shed
A skin of shit and scum,
And glinted through the fretted bridge,
Gold as Byzantium.

> Then suddenly the sun was snuffed
> Behind a sooty cloud,
> And night let fall on Glasgow Green
> Its sulphur-stinking shroud . . .

And there used to be the notorious Gorbals slums. Alexander McArthur's novel *No Mean City* laid them bare:

> Battles and sex are the only free diversions in slum life. Couple them with drink,
> which costs money, and you have the three principal outlets for that escape
> complex which is for ever working in the tenement dweller's subconscious mind.

The city fathers didn't care for this image of Glasgow, and in classic fashion, rather than improving the housing, they banned the book. Naturally this did no harm to its sales, and for nearly thirty years *No Mean City* seemed to be the only fictional Glasgow landscape available.

In the 1960s, everything changed. The Gorbals slums (along with much else) were knocked down. Edwin Morgan's Glasgow poetry breathes the renewal and excitement first felt in that heady decade:

> . . . green May, and the slow great blocks rising
> under yellow tower cranes, concrete and glass and steel
> out of a dour rubble it was and barefoot children gone –
> Is it only the slow stirring, a city's renewed life
> that stirs me, could it stir me so deeply
> as May, but could May have stirred
> what I feel of desire and strength
> like an arm saluting a sun?

It was a time of improvement in many ways, but something good was lost too, as people were moved from the city centre and long-settled residential areas to outlying housing schemes. Jeff Torrington's novel *Swing Hammer Swing!*, set in the very same Gorbals, makes that clear:

> Having so cursorily dismantled the community's heart, that sooty reciprocating
> engine, admittedly an antique clapped-out affair, but one that'd been nevertheless
> capable of generating amazing funds of human warmth, they'd bundled it off into
> the asylum of history . . .

And out of these changes, good and bad, came a new kind of Glasgow writing. Archie Hind with his novel *The Dear Green Place*; Alasdair Gray with *Lanark*; Tom Leonard and his unsparing poetry; Liz Lochhead, writing both poetry and drama; and first among equals, perhaps, James Kelman, who won the Booker Prize with *How Late it Was, How Late*. Kelman's work grows from Glasgow soil – there is no doubt that it's about Glasgow – yet there's hardly any topographical description in his novels and short stories. Rather he presents the city, its atmosphere and its people, in such a way that 'Kelman's Glasgow' becomes a place on the map.

Glasgow writing continues. Donny O'Rourke is only one of a cavalcade of recent poets who rejoice in the infinite variety of city life:

> . . . God Glasgow it's glorious
> just to gulp you down in heartfuls,
> feeling something quite like love.

That's Glasgow, as it could be any living city. One of Morgan's *Glasgow Sonnets* sees the city as a living organism indeed:

> It groans and shakes, contracts and grows again.
> Its giant broken shoulders shrug off rain.
> It digs its pits to a shauchling refrain.
> Roadworks and graveyards like their gallus men.
> It fattens fires and murders in a pen
> and lets them out in flaps and squalls of pain.
> It sometimes tears its smoky counterpane
> to hoist a bleary fist at nothing, then
> at everything, you never know. The west
> could still be laid with no one's tears like dust
> and barricaded windows be the best
> to see from till the shops, the ships, the trust
> return like thunder. Give the Clyde the rest.
> Man and the sea make cities as they must.

The Scottish city, shaped by its past, reaching for its future: a place of buildings and people and work and play, growing in the landscape, in the place where it belongs.

III
The Other Landscape

13 Fingalian Places

After *Cill Osbran* closed up to Closeburn
more books were shut than Osbran's psalter.
Seeking to baptize the new born name
the pedants hurried to the nearest water
which wasn't even warm.

William Neill

Behind the mountains and glens, behind the farms and small towns and cities, there's another landscape of Scotland. It is inhabited, in our minds, by other people, who don't quite fit into everyday life.

These people, over the years, may have been in touch with something beyond the visible landscape, and could be called psychics, or perhaps saints. They may have been able to see farther ahead in time than their neighbours, or deeper into the meaning of things, and so got the name of prophets. Some of them, almost certainly, were never there at all. Still they have left their names and their legends as traces on the land.

All over Scotland there are such traces of the Fianna, followers of the mythical hunter and warrior Fionn mac Cumhaill, or Finn MacCool. They were based in Ireland, but their forays and adventures, both warlike and romantic, evidently led them far and wide. So we have Suidhe Fhinn, Fionn's seat, above Portree in Skye, where Fionn sat to watch his warriors hunting. Coire Cath nam Fionn in the Cairngorms is 'the corrie of the battle of the Fianna', and above it is Beinn Bhrotain, named for Brodan, Fionn's hound. Fèinne-bheinn, above Loch Hope in Sutherland, and Stob an Fhainne at Inversnaid on Loch Lomond are other Fingalian hills.

Whenever you find Ben Gulbin – there are several, and Yeats's Ben Bulben in County Sligo has the same name – it may be the site where the hero Diarmid, his lover Grainne (whom he stole from the ageing Fionn) and their two hounds are buried. They hunted the torc, or boar (and Diarmid was killed by a boar, though there was magic involved), and so there's often a nearby 'boar hill' like Carn an Tuirc.

Fingal's Cave on Staffa gives us a slightly different message. Fingal is Fionn, but the form Fingal became popular in Scotland only in the eighteenth century, when James Macpherson went travelling in the Highlands in search of the lost epics of ancient Gaelic literature. On his return he published two volumes which were presented as translations from the work of the bard Ossian, son of Fingal, and sparked great enthusiasm for what became known as the Ossianic legends. Fingal's Cave was promptly named, and Ossian's birthplace in Glencoe and his grave in the Sma' Glen near Crieff were identified. Wordsworth, touring the Highlands, was quite affected by his visit to this site:

> In this still place, remote from men,
> Sleeps Ossian, in the *Narrow Glen*; . . .
> He sang of battles, and the breath
> Of stormy war, and violent death; . . .
> But this is calm; there cannot be
> A more entire tranquillity.

But not everyone was convinced that the material published by Macpherson was genuinely Ossianic. He spoke of finding ancient manuscripts, but was never able to produce any for inspection. Dr Johnson was of the opinion that Macpherson 'found names, and stories, and phrases, nay passages in old songs, and with them has blended his own compositions, and so made what he gives to the world as the translation of an ancient poem.' (Modern scholars tend to agree with this.) If he hadn't been silly enough to mention manuscripts, Johnson considered, Macpherson might have got away with it. Now that the dust has settled it's probably possible to appreciate how Macpherson did draw the attention of his world – a very different place from that distant, romantic, golden age – to to the great, mysterious figures of Fionn and the Fianna, hunting and fighting and loving.

The real Ossian (if he existed), together with Fionn's nephew Cailte, survived, it's said, into the Christian era. They went to meet St Patrick (who is a slightly more historical figure, though truth and legend still intertwine in stories of his life) and, according to the legend, heated discussions took place. Patrick, the great missionary saint, tried to convert Ossian and Cailte, while the Celtic heroes argued the case for their pagan but liberal and joyous way of life against the holy conformity of Christianity.

There's also a story that St Kentigern baptised the enchanter Merlin in the wild woods of Tweeddale. Perhaps we can see a picture here: Scotland at the meeting-point of two cultures, two systems of belief. The struggle was a long one. As late as the sixteenth century John Carswell, bishop of the Isles, was complaining about 'composers and writers and patrons of Gaelic, [who] prefer vain hurtful lying worldly tales about the heroes and Fionn mac Cumhaill and his warriors . . . rather than to write and compose and to preserve the very Word of God.'

On the whole, however, Christianity won. To judge by the many saint-connected placenames, the ruined chapels and holy wells that cover the countryside, there must have been a few hundred years when saints were as thick on the ground as the Fingalian heroes had previously been. At times we can see the overlap. On Skye, on Lewis, on South Uist and elsewhere there are pre-Christian standing stones and wells, together with chapels, at places called Kilbride, because St Bride or Brigid, a powerful figure in the Celtic church, took over many of her duties from the pagan goddess also called Bride. Both are patrons of fire, fertility, poetry, beauty. Both are also concerned with cattle. One of the many songs in *Carmina Gadelica*, collected in the Western Isles where Bride was particularly revered, runs:

Brighde nan gealachos,
Brighde na bìth,
Brighde nan gealabhos,
Brighde na nì.

Brigit of the white feet,
Brigit of calmness,
Brigit of the white palms,
Brigit of the kine.

The poor man in Sir David Lyndsay's sixteenth-century drama *Satyre of the Thrie Estaites*, whose cows have been removed by a cruel landlord, equally knows who will help him: 'Saint Bride, Saint Bride, send me my kye again!'

Meanwhile St Ninian, the first missionary to Scotland, had established his monastery – Candida Casa, the white house – at what is now Whithorn in Wigtownshire, and his name, in one version or another, recurs all the way from Galloway to St Ninian's Isle in Shetland. Ninian is said to have consecrated the first burying-ground in Glasgow, but the saint who took over there was Kentigern, sometimes known as Mungo (a nickname, apparently, meaning 'dear little dog', because his official name meant 'hound-lord'.)

Certainly Kentigern has left his mark all over Glasgow. On buildings, on streetlamps, on bin-lorries you see his symbols in the city's coat of arms, and everyone knows the traditional rhyme:

There's the tree that never grew,
There's the bird that never flew,
There's the bell that never rang,
There's the fish that never swam.

This is all from the legend of Kentigern's life, in which he caused a dead branch to burst into flame and restored a dead robin to life, and rang the bell to call people to prayer. The salmon became involved when Kentigern rescued a queen from the consequences of her own folly. Her jealous husband had demanded to see the ring he had given her, which unfortunately she had passed on to a lover. Following Kentigern's instructions, she found the ring safe inside one of the salmon which used to frequent the river Clyde.

Edwin Morgan gracefully uses the further legend of a meeting between two saints, Kentigern of Glasgow and Columba of Iona:

> . . . The cell
> is filled with song. Outside, *puer cantat*.
> *Veni venator* sings the gallus kern.
> The saints dip startled cups in Mungo's well.

Columba, or Colum Cille – dove of the church – came from Ireland, possibly exiled after a dispute (the stories, as so often, vary). Several times his coracle put in at a likely-looking spot on the west coast of Scotland, but at each place Columba found that Ireland could still be seen, and so he sailed on. Finally he reached the island of Iona, landing at a small bay on the south coast which is now called Port a' Churaich, the port of the coracle. Nearby is the hill Càrn Cùl ri Eirinn, 'the hill with its back to Ireland'. From here the Irish coast could no longer be seen, and Columba, so it's said, knew he had reached the right place.

Columba established a monastic settlement here, though the nunnery whose ruins can be seen dates from long after his time. The offshore Eilean nam Ban, 'isle of the women', may have been reserved for the wives of laymen employed on Iona. According to tradition Columba banished them there, together with their cows, because 'Far am bi bò bidh bean, 's far am bi bean bidh mallachadh – Where there will be a cow there will be a woman, and where there will be a woman there will be trouble.' He seems to have foreseen that the cows would eventually get in:

> I mo chridhe, I mo ghràidh
> An àite guth manaich bidh geum bà
> Ach man dig an saoghal gu crìch
> Bidh I mar a bhà.

> In Iona of my heart, Iona of my love,
> Instead of monks' voices will be the lowing of cattle;
> But ere the world come to an end
> Iona shall be as it was.

Though the buildings on Iona, and even the beautiful carved crosses, date from long after Columba, there are places on the island which he must have known. On Cnoc nan Aingeal, the hill of the angels, he is said to have conversed with heavenly messengers. (By now it's no surprise to find that this hillock is also known as Sìthean Mòr, the big fairy hill.) On Tòrr an Aba, the hill of the abbot, rough stone foundations can be seen, answering the ancient descriptions of Columba's cell, where he slept, we are told, on the bare rock.

Perhaps this was where he wrote *Altus Prosator* (*The Maker on High*), the oldest known Scottish poem. There are twenty-three stanzas, each beginning with a different letter of the alphabet, which Edwin Morgan has translated from the original Latin: 'Ancient exalted seed-scatterer whom time gave no progenitor . . .'

Monks from Iona carried Christianity far and wide, and so all over Scotland we find the names Inchcolm, Kirkcolm, Kilcolmkeil, where churches were founded by Columba's followers or dedicated to him. Again we can sometimes see what used to be there. A rock near Dunaverty in Kintyre bearing the carved shapes of two feet, known locally as St Columba's Footprints, is said to be one of the places where the saint looked back to Ireland (which is certainly in clear view, only a few miles away). One footstep has been cut in relatively recent times, but the other probably marks a sacred site, like Dunadd farther north, where a Celtic chieftain, symbolically standing in the footsteps of his predecessors, took his oath of office. Once again a veil of Christianity has been drawn across the older culture that the missionaries found.

Seven hundred years after Columba, though, a memory of that culture still survived. The Borders wizard, Michael Scot, born towards the end of the twelfth century, went abroad to get his education, and when he came back was held to be not merely learned but a master of magical powers. He lived, it's said, at Aikwood Tower in Ettrickdale, which provides some episodes for James Hogg's novel *Three Perils of Man*. Helped by elvish servants, he 'bridled the Tweed with a curb of stone' (in more prosaic terms, perhaps he constructed a weir or dam). Most famously, it was his spell which cleft the Eildon Hills in three, as anyone can see them to this day. He is said to be buried in Melrose Abbey, and though this, like the rest of his life, is historically uncertain, Walter Scott had no doubts:

> Buried on St Michael's night,
> When the bell toll'd one, and the moon was bright,
> Whose chamber was dug among the dead,
> When the floor of the chancel was stained red.

Similarly, a century later than Michael Scot, Thomas the Rhymer of Ercildoune – now Earlston – may have written verse. (Some think that his surname was Learmont and that he was an ancestor of the Russian poet Lermontov.) But he became known not just as a poet but as a prophet. He foretold the exploits of Robert the Bruce, the Union of the Crowns, and the future, good and bad, of some of the great Border families: 'Tide what may betide, Haig shall be Haig of Bemersyde.'

Certainly everyone knows that Thomas met the Queen of the Fairies at the Eildon Tree, and went with her through a secret passage under the Eildon Hills:

> It was mirk mirk night, there was nae stern light,
> And they waded in red blude to the knee;
> For a' the blude that's shed on earth
> Rins through the springs o' that countrie.

Thomas lived in Fairyland for seven years. Then he was allowed to return home, with the gift of a tongue that could never lie, and made his predictions, which were perceived to come true. It's easy for us, in hindsight, to see how such a legend could have gathered round a young man who returned to his native village after several years away, appearing to know everything (or at least more than the stay-at-homes knew) about the mysteries of life. Where could he have got this knowledge? Well, there's something distinctly uncanny about the triple-peaked Eildon Hills – as any traveller in the Borders will agree – so it must have been there.

Something similar, we may think, accounts for the reputation of the Brahan Seer, Coinneach Odhar Fiosaiche – brown-haired Kenneth the Knowledgeable – who lived in the seventeenth century, well within what we might consider enlightened times. He predicted the time when there would be 'a road on every hill and a bridge on every stream', but anybody could predict that. A clever man with an eye for scientific and engineering possibilities might foresee 'a black bridleless horse passing through Muir of Ord' (the railway) or 'full-rigged ships sailing behind the hill of Tomnahurich' (the Caledonian Canal). A politically-minded man might even have foreseen Culloden: 'Oh Drummossie, before many generations have passed your bleak moor will be stained with the best blood of the Highlands.' (Though, given that the Highlanders surprised experts at the time by choosing the highly unsuitable Drummossie Moor for their battlefield, the location predicted by Coinneach Odhar is unnervingly precise.)

Similarly explicable, up to a point, is the Brahan Seer's prediction of the Clearances and the consequent emigration. 'The jawbone of the sheep will put the plough on the rafters . . . The whole Highlands will become one huge deer-forest . . . The people will leave for islands yet unknown.' All perfectly predictable by a shrewd man, until the sting in the tail: 'The deer and other wild animals will be exterminated by black rain.' That didn't make much sense to anybody until nuclear fallout and pollution began to appear in the news.

Astute and far-seeing Coinneach Odhar may have been, but he wasn't a tactful man. Summoned by the Countess of Seaforth for news of her husband who was abroad on business, the Seer reported that the Earl was perfectly well, in a splendid room in Paris, with his arm round the waist of a beautiful young lady. That wasn't exactly what the Countess wanted to hear, and she ordered Coinneach's immediate execution in a barrel of burning tar.

Before he died the Seer made his grimmest and most detailed prediction of all. The end of the House of Seaforth was soon to come, in the time of a chief who was deaf and dumb, and whose neighbouring lairds at the time were respectively buck-toothed, hare-lipped, feeble-minded and stammering. Seaforth's four sons would die before him. His estate would be inherited by 'a white-hooded lassie from the east', and she would kill her sister. The prophecy was known all over the district before Coinneach Odhar was long dead.

The Brahan Seer is more securely anchored in history than the Fianna, Michael Scot or Thomas the Rhymer. The site of his execution on the Black Isle is marked with a stone and there, looking over the landscape he knew and the changes he may have foreseen, it's fairly easy to rationalise away his predictions. Maybe he was, after all, just smarter than the Countess of Seaforth.

But a hundred and fifty years after Coinneach's death – not long in the story of the Highlands – the Seaforth line did come to an end. The last chief and his neighbours at the time were afflicted as Coinneach had described. The sons predeceased their father, and the heiress's sister died. The Brahan Seer had got every detail right, and no one has ever quite been able to explain how he did that.

14 On the Road

That ribbon of smoke
across the valley
is a road we climb.

Sean Rafferty

It's quite unusual now, but sometimes they can still be seen on the road, a raggle-taggle band of men and women and shy children, clearly a family group with their high cheekbones, their weatherbeaten faces and sun-bleached hair. These are the travelling people of Scotland. You might come across a campsite, though in the industrialised, car-oriented countryside of today these are disgracefully few. Duncan Williamson, born in a tent on Lochfyneside in Argyll and now a traditional storyteller and a well-respected authority on travellers, has seen things change:

> O come all youse hawkers, you men of the road,
> Youse hawkers who wander around,
> My story is sad, for it saddens my heart,
> For they've closed all our campin grounds down.

There will be caravans on the site rather than the bow tents, the gellies and barricades, and as well as the genuine travellers today there's likely to be an uneasy mixture of pedlars, New Agers and drop-outs, rousing local residents to rage. House-dwellers have never been too keen on travelling people, whom they tend to call 'tinkers'. That only means 'tinsmith', a traditional traveller occupation, but it became, in common speech, a nasty insult. ('Look at you, you're like a tinker! You dirty tink!') The travellers themselves have never liked the term and it is not an acceptable description now. Hearing it, you get a sudden chilling glimpse of the house-dwellers' mindset. George Mackay Brown's poem 'Tinkers' moves from his view of the exotic visitors to that of the judgmental people of the town:

> Princes, they ruled in our street
> A long shining age,
> While Merran peeped through her curtains
> Like a hawk from a cage.
>
> Paupers, they filthied our pier
> A piece of one afternoon,
> Then scowled, stank, shouldered their packs
> And cursed and were gone.

The travellers have been part of Scotland's life and landscape for a very long time. Exactly how long is a difficult question. John Galt's eighteenth-century minister in *Annals of the Parish* knows about them:

> . . . a gang of tinklers, that made horn-spoons and mended bellows. Where they
> came from never was well made out, but being a blackavised crew, they were
> generally thought to be Egyptians. They tarried about a week among us, living
> in tents, with their little ones squattling among the litter; and one of the older
> men of them set and tempered to me two razors, that were as good as nothing,
> but which he made better than when they were new.

Walter Scott as a child saw Madge Gordon, the queen of the Yetholm gipsies, and based the character Meg
Merrilies in his novel *Guy Mannering* on her. The king or queen belonged to the ancient gipsy family of Faa
(who claimed that the name had come down from their ancestors, the Pharaohs) and coronations were held
on the green at Kirk Yetholm, which used to be the gipsy capital of Scotland.

But gipsies are not the same as tinkers. In stories, and in the popular mind, there's a certain air of romance
about gipsies, seen as lovable rogues and vagabonds:

> The gipsies they came to Lord Cassillis' yett,
> And O! but they sang bonnie;
> They sang sae sweet, and sae complete,
> That down came our fair Ladie . . .
>
> By and by came home this noble Lord,
> And asking for his ladie,
> The one did cry, the other did reply,
> 'She is gone with the gipsy laddie.'

The Yetholm gipsies were quite distinct from the travelling people who followed Highland roads. They certainly
favoured different areas of Scotland for their campsites and their traditional routes, and probably came from
different stock.

Where the Highland travellers came from, and when they appeared, no one is sure. It has been suggested that
they are the descendants of prehistoric hunter-gatherers, or else of a respected caste of specialist metal-workers,
swordsmiths to Celtic princes. Another romantic theory is that they are descendants of the broken clans forced
into hiding after Culloden. Or they're MacGregors, outlawed for various exploits or crimes, like their famous leader
Rob Roy. In that case, the legend continues, perhaps they are of royal descent, born on the wrong side of the blanket
to one of those poetic wandering Stewart kings, as the motto of Clan Gregor proudly claims: ''S Rioghal mo Dhream,
my race is royal'. None of this, of course, is possible to prove. To the comfort of all, it's equally hard to disprove.

It's true that Stewart is a traveller name. The recurrence of clan or family names among travellers is very marked, and different families are linked to different areas of Scotland: Stewarts are found in Perthshire and Sutherland, Williamsons in Wester Ross and Argyll, Townsleys in Kintyre, among many more. MacPhee is sometimes regarded as the oldest traveller clan, its members being considered rather unlucky to deal with, slightly uncanny. That's because their name could indicate that they are descended from the people of the fairy hills. Even if we forget about an other-worldly ancestry, traveller relationships are complicated, with kinship up and down and across generations. There are, or used to be, a few old people who, like the griots of West Africa, carried the whole family tree in their heads.

If there's one thing that house-dwellers do know, or think they do, it's that travellers have a language of their own, 'the cant'. It used to be heard as the carts and ponies straggled through the douce streets of a country town, rapidly spoken, quite incomprehensible to the bystander. While it may not be a full language, it is certainly a secret tongue, composed of words from many sources which have been borrowed and adopted as travellers moved through Europe and beyond.

Everyday Scots speech has in its turn adopted a few cant words, like 'barrie', meaning good, or 'gadgie', a man; but that isn't the key to using the cant. Its secret lies not in the words, but in the way they are spoken or employed, as Betsy Whyte, born a Perthshire traveller, has explained:

> One word could have many meanings and could carry the meaning of a whole sentence, depending on the situation and the tone of voice. In fact, a traveller could appear to be having a normal conversation with a non-traveller – but in reality be giving a message, perhaps a warning, to any traveller listening . . .
> We can *tell* the words to anyone, but *how* to use them is something which will be lost once the travellers of this generation are gone.

More generally, house-dwellers came into contact with travellers when they turned up on the doorstep selling their wares: milk cans, saucepans and kettles, baskets woven from hazel or willow wands, pot-scrubbers from tough heather roots. Some families were pearl-fishers, using a glass-bottomed jug to see through the water and a split-ended rod to grip the mussels which might hold pearls. Casual farmwork – cutting hay, shawing turnips, tattie-howking – was available as the seasons turned and as the travellers followed the road.

Each summer the berry-picking at Blairgowrie, 'the berry-fields o' Blair', provided a rendezvous for travellers from all over Scotland, a time of hard work but also of reunions, conversations, songs and stories. Traveller culture has been called 'the third great zone of Scottish folk culture', alongside the ballads and the Gaelic

heritage. The description is by Hamish Henderson, who began collecting traveller songs and stories in the 1950s and found that:

> . . . the oral literature and song of the Travelling People was probably not only
> the most substantially ancient but also the most vital of all Scotland's various,
> towering folk traditions . . . Magnificent folk riches [lay], totally unregarded and
> essentially unknown, among that traditionally maligned group, 'the Tinkers',
> the Travelling People.

Singers like Jeannie Robertson, storytellers like Duncan Williamson and Stanley Robertson, and many more, have proved to be in touch with a great treasure-house of lore, the oldest traditions still part of their lives. As a small boy Williamson and his brothers and sisters were sternly warned to leave standing stones, 'the Pictish Stones', alone:

> We were allowed to look at them, admire them. But we could not even put a hand
> on them . . . Father had said, 'These stones belong to your people, your people
> a long time ago. They put them there for a purpose, so that you would remember
> them.' . . . And Father would always make sure he would camp not far from some
> of the great Standing Stones. He would have no fear of burkers [body-snatchers],
> no fear of ghosts and spirits that many people had in these days. He felt safe,
> as if that giant stone were looking over, guarding us children.

Since traveller culture itself is so rich, perhaps it doesn't matter if outsiders struggle to express the ethos of this life. Scottish writers, who tend to be of the house-dwelling sort, don't always have great success in depicting the travelling people. The death in Violet Jacob's poem 'The Last o' the Tinkler' is a sentimental moment:

> There's jist the tent to leave, lad,
> I've gaithered little gear,
> There's jist yersel' to grieve, lad,
> An' the auld dog here . . .

Ikey, a recurrent character in the poems of George Mackay Brown, is a slightly stylised vagrant:

> Rognvald who stalks round Corse with his stick
> I do not love.
> His dog has a loud sharp mouth.
> The wood of his door is very hard.

Once, tangled in his barbed wire
(I was paying respect to his hens, stroking a wing)
He laid his stick on me.
That was out of a hard forest also.

But Naomi Mitchison, who championed the cause of the travellers in real life, managed to express some of their problems in fiction:

> . . . Mostly all the tinker children came to my school in winter, maybe two terms, but then they would be on the road again, all summer, everything they had learned from me forgotten . . . Maybe they were learning another set of things on the roads the travellers took . . . My children would never sit next the tinks. It was the smell off them, you understand, wood smoke and little washing, with no soap. But if you lived the way the travelling folk used to, you'd not have much chance of looking a bath in the face.

There are more and different problems now. In recent years, the situation of the travelling people has become sadly precarious. Land is now so intensively used, whether farmed or built on, that the open countryside once available for camps and journeys has shrunk to a fraction of its former welcoming breadth. Traditional skills are no longer needed. Duncan Williamson has noted:

> . . . The demand for tin dishes fell away with the coming of aluminium goods to the market. Before the end of the Second World War my father buried all his tinmaking tools, which had belonged to his father. He wouldn't show us where he'd buried them, because he felt they were too precious to be lost or destroyed.

Because of mechanisation, casual farmwork is in short supply. Some travellers have taken up more urban occupations like scrap-dealing, but not everyone has been able to adapt, and a kind of demoralisation has been added to health and economic problems.

Commissions have been set up to consider the question of the travelling people, and reports have acknowledged the unique value of this ancient lifestyle and culture. It's agreed that there should be housing for those who want to settle down and suitable campsites for those who want to keep up the travelling way of life, but nothing seems to happen very quickly. The future is hard to predict, but Scotland's landscape and life will be much poorer if the travellers disappear.

15 A Cold Ceilidh

I do not much like extermination carried out
so thoroughly and on system – it seems bad policy.

Hugh Miller

The Highland Clearances, beginning late in the eighteenth century and continuing until the mid-nineteenth, left deep scars on Scotland. Basically the story is simple: communities of crofters were evicted, to make way, generally, for large-scale sheep farming, a more profitable use of the land. In strict legal terms the landowners had every right to carry out the evictions, as Neil Gunn makes a character explain blandly in his novel *Butcher's Broom*:

> Those people who were cleared by you off the Larg sheep farm – well, naturally
> they have a sense of grievance. Anybody who loses anything has a sense of
> grievance. I mean, that will pass. It's only temporary and, in a way, natural
> enough. After all, you have been very kind to them. There was no obligation
> upon the estate to do anything for them. The land is absolutely his lordship's,
> to do with as he likes.

Possibly the landowners meant well, or convinced themselves that they did. The idea, as presented, was that the crofters would be provided with new occupations, such as fishing, and attain a better quality of life. But in Sutherland, for instance, the people cleared from glens like Strath Naver and the Strath of Kildonan were awkwardly settled along the coast, having no experience or skills in the new work which they were expected to take up. Hugh Miller, the Cromarty geologist and writer who saw the process going on, puts it clearly enough:

> The interior of [Sutherland] was thus *improved* into a desert . . . The county
> has not been depopulated – its population has been merely arranged after
> a new fashion. The late Duchess found it spread equally over the interior and
> the sea-coast, and in very comfortable circumstances; she left it compressed into
> a wretched selvage of poverty and suffering that fringes the county on its eastern
> and western shores.

And the better life never came about. The fishing and other imported industries failed to thrive. Adam Drinan pictures the plight of the Highlanders in his verse play *The Ghosts of the Strath*:

> Now down on the shore the voice
>   was a jeering gull's,
> where men and women dibbled
>   in shells and dulse
> to maintain themselves, like silly sea-pies,
>   on mussels.

Sleeping beneath bushes,

      they scratched pebbly fields.

Risking their lives, they kept alive

      by fishing.

And the rich in fake kilts rested from their labours . . .

Many of the evicted moved on again, south to the cities or out to America, far from the glens. There's a painting, sentimental in the Victorian style but none the less evocative, which shows a family setting sail for America, while the aged grandfather, too frail for the journey, is left on the shore. The painter, Thomas Faed, called it 'The Last of the Clan'.

Out of the evictions came stories of brutality, the villain of the piece frequently being Patrick Sellar, the factor for the Sutherland estates. Some of the accusations at least were backed by eye-witness reports, like the one which has Sellar being told of a bedridden old woman too frail to leave her house. 'Damn her, the old witch,' said Sellar, 'she has lived too long, let her burn,' and she was carried out of her torched cottage with her blankets already in flames. She died within five days. Sellar was charged with culpable homicide and brought to trial, but he was acquitted. 'Take into account the character of the accused,' the judge loftily directed the jury, and apparently they took the hint as it was meant, for Sellar was a respectable man.

It's no wonder that Scottish writers have taken up this theme. As well as *Butcher's Broom*, the classic novels of the clearances are Fionn MacColla's *And the Cock Crew* and Iain Crichton Smith's *Consider the Lilies*. MacColla's central character is the minister Maighstir Sachairi. Highland ministers were often blamed for failing to support their flock against the landowners, and Sachairi shares that indictment, but goes beyond it into a crisis of tortured conscience. Iain Crichton Smith's novel is a fictional study of one old woman – he insisted that it wasn't a work of historical scholarship – but again we confront the role of the church, its repressive influence and mind-shaping authority (which Crichton Smith saw as still present in his own time). We may think of the words scratched on a windowpane in Croick parish church, in a remote glen in Easter Ross, by families who sheltered in the churchyard – they weren't allowed into the church itself – after their eviction in 1845. 'Glencalvie people the wicked generation,' they have written in their despair, convinced by their grim creed that it must all be their own fault.

A cold lasting anger about the Clearances is still to be found in the Highlands. It comes out in the work of modern Gaelic poets like Derick Thomson:

A Shrath Nabhair 's a Shrath Chill Donnain,
is beag an t-iongnadh ged a chinneadh am fraoch àlainn oirbh,
a' falach nan lotan a dh' fhàg Pàdraig Sellar 's a sheòrsa . . .

O Strathnaver and Strath of Kildonan
it is little wonder that the heather should bloom on your slopes
hiding the wounds that Patrick Sellar, and such as he, made . . .

Sellar's name is still reviled and there's a continuing debate about the statue of the Duke of Sutherland which stands on a hilltop above Golspie. Should it be pulled down, or should it stay as a lasting reminder of what was done? Iain Crichton Smith looks to an even more bitterly satisfying revenge:

The thistles climb the thatch. Forever
this sharp scale in our poems,
as also the waste music of the sea.

The stars shine over Sutherland
in a cold ceilidh of their own,
as, in the morning, the silver cane

cropped among corn. We will remember this.
Though hate is evil we cannot
but hope your courtier's heels in hell

are burning: that to hear
the thatch sizzling in tanged smoke
your hot ears slowly learn.

There is more to the story than two glens in Sutherland and a short spell of brutality. Evictions went on for many years and in many parts of the Highlands. Uilleam MacDhùnlèibhe (William Livingstone) wrote of what he saw in nineteenth-century Islay:

Ged thig ànrach aineoil
Gus a' chala, 's e sa cheò,
Chan fhaic e soills on chagailt
Air a' chladach so nas mò;

Chuir gamhlas Ghall air fuadach
Na tha bhuainn 's nach till gu bràth,
Mar a fhuair 's a chunnaic mise:
Thoir am fios so chun a' Bhàird.

Though a stranger, in his wanderings
comes to harbour in the mist,
The hearth has no light shining
any more upon this coast;
For Lowland spite has scattered
those who will not come again;
will you carry this clear message,
as I see it, to the Bard.

Sometimes the story is one of emigration forced by economic necessity, but none the less heartbreaking for that. Neil Munro returns to Glen Aora in Argyll, where he was brought up, to find 'the hearth-stone's black and cold.' Everything is sadly changed: 'And sturdy grows the nettle,' he writes, 'on the place beloved of old.'

The greatest poem of the desolate Highlands is Sorley MacLean's 'Hallaig'. Hallaig is – or was – a township on the island of Raasay, off Skye, which Boswell and Johnson had visited during their tour in 1773. 'Very good grass-fields and corn-lands,' they noted, 'abundance of black cattle, sheep and goats . . . black-cock in extraordinary abundance, moor-fowl, plover and wild pigeons.' They saw women waulking tweed, and joined in the evening's dancing. 'The gaiety of the scene was such,' wrote Boswell, 'that I for a moment doubted whether unhappiness had any place in Raasay.'

But the island, with all its townships, was cleared for sheep-farming in the 1850s, and most of the people had to emigrate overseas. A hundred years later Sorley MacLean, himself born on Raasay, began his poem with the haunting image: 'Tha tìm, am fiadh, an coille Hallaig/Time, the deer, is in the wood of Hallaig.'

Mura tig 's ann theàrnas mi a Hallaig
a dh' ionnsaigh sàbaid nam marbh,
far a bheil an sluagh a' tathaich,
gach aon ghinealach a dh' fhalbh.

Tha iad fhathast ann a Hallaig,
Clann Ghill-Eain 's Clann Mhic Leòid,
na bh' ann ri linn Mhic Ghille Chaluim:
chunnacas na mairbh beò.

. . . I will go down to Hallaig,
to the Sabbath of the dead,
where the people are frequenting,
every single generation gone.

They are still in Hallaig,
MacLeans and MacLeods,
all who were there in the time of Mac Gille Chaluim:
the dead have been seen alive.

Emigration from Scotland became a fact of life, and, less dramatic but just as damaging, there has been a general movement of people away from the Highlands, including the Western and Northern Isles, to industrial areas. George Mackay Brown sees the effects in the beautiful valley of Rackwick on the Orkney island of Hoy:

At Burnmouth the door hangs from a broken hinge
And the fire is out.

The windows of Shore empty sockets
And the hearth coldness.

At Bunertoon the small drains are choked.
Thrushes sing in the chimney . . .

Some of the causes, beginning with the historical Clearances but continuing into the present day, are explored in John McGrath's ceilidh-play *The Cheviot, the Stag, and the Black, Black Oil*, first performed in 1973. There's the shooting and fishing culture for which great swathes of hills and rivers have been dedicated to a few months of sport:

Oh it's awfully, frightfully nice,
Shooting stags, my dear, and grice –
And there's nothing quite so right
As a fortnight catching trite:

> And if the locals should complain,
> Well we can clear them off again.

There's the exploitation of the Highlands for tourist purposes: 'Picture it, if yous will,' offers the entrepreneur Andy McChuckemup, 'a drive-in clachan on every hill-top where formerly there was hee-haw but scenery.' There's the parcelling out of Scotland among absentee landlords and multi-national corporations; and (since by the 1970s the effects of the North Sea oil boom had already become all too apparent) there's the oil:

> Take your oil-rigs by the score,
> Drill a little well just a little off-shore,
> Pipe that oil in from the sea,
> Pipe those profits home to me.

'Aye, one thing's certain,' say McGrath's crofter and his wife, 'we can't live here.'

A poem by Allan Ramsay, dating from an earlier age of wandering Scots, had become the anthem of the Clearances:

> Farewell to Lochaber, and farewell my Jean,
> Where heartsome wi' thee I've mony days been;
> For Lochaber no more, Lochaber no more,
> We'll maybe return to Lochaber no more.

In recent years the pop group The Proclaimers, Craig and Charlie Reid, have brought things up to date in their song 'Letter from America'. Deliberately they recall the eighteenth-century poem and the nineteenth-century evictions, but the placenames they use are those notorious for some of the many factory closures in Scotland during the late twentieth century:

> Bathgate no more
> Linwood no more
> Methil no more
> Irvine no more . . .

The process of depopulation and emigration from Scotland which began at the time of the Clearances, and has featured in Scottish writing ever since, is far from over yet.

16 In the Heather

Now we ran among the birches,
now stooping behind low humps upon the mountain side;
now crawling on all fours among the heather.
The pace was deadly; my heart seemed bursting against my ribs;
and I had neither time to think nor breath to speak with.

Robert Louis Stevenson

All broad Scotland: it's an old phrase and a glorious idea. When it was coined, most people in Scotland lived in a huddle of houses, farmstead or village or town. But outside the farmyard, a step from the street, beyond the town wall, stretched the moors and the glens. If you had come into conflict with the rules of the community, or, just as likely, with the self-important people who administered them, then you could 'take to the heather', where a different set of rules applied. Evasion, flight, escape, are all part of Scotland's landscape.

So are the outlaws and fugitives themselves, whether they belong to real life or fiction, or whether one has, over the years, merged with the other. It's not easy, for instance, to sort out the historical Rob Roy MacGregor, operating as a drover with excursions into cattle-rustling at the turn of the eighteenth century, from the legendary brigand whose mementoes fill the tourist shops of the Trossachs, or to determine the connection between either of them and Sir Walter Scott's novel *Rob Roy*.

Historically, Rob Roy – red-haired Rob – was born in Glengyle at the head of Loch Katrine in 1671. A third son, he was granted the land of Craigrostan on the eastern shore of Loch Lomond, and might have made a perfectly good living from the peaceful occupation of cattle-trading. But he is remembered as a landless outlaw, a sort of Scottish Robin Hood. It's certain that he did carry out cattle raids, that he was bankrupted and his house was burned, that he was arrested and escaped more than once. What happened?

It's a complicated story, full of rumours, accusations and counter-claims. Even before Rob Roy's time Clan Gregor, the Children of the Mist, had been outlawed and persecuted for reasons connected with the ambitions of Clan Campbell, so that MacGregors had enemies in high places. But the accounts of Rob Roy's exploits in particular seem to have caught the imagination of the English writer Daniel Defoe on visits to Scotland. He recounted them in print in a colourful and largely fictionalised style. These stories were still current when Scott was researching for his novel, and, less than a hundred years after Rob Roy's death, he found plenty of informants who knew all about the local hero. Scott used what they told him uncritically, and somewhere about here the legends begin.

So, in the Trossachs today, you can't get away from Rob Roy. We can see Eilean Dearg, the island in Loch Katrine where Rob held the Duke of Montrose's factor prisoner; Rob Roy's Prison near Rowardennan, a rocky outcrop where (we are told) he amused himself by lowering captives into the chilly waters of Loch Lomond; and Rob Roy's Grave in the churchyard at Balquhidder. Wordsworth wrote a poem about this:

> Then clear the weeds from off his grave,
> And let us chaunt a passing stave
> In honour of that Outlaw brave.

Unfortunately, his weed-clearing efforts were misdirected. Like many a tourist, he had been misdirected or misinformed, and was admiring a grave in another MacGregor burial ground, some miles away. Even in Balquhidder things are not straightforward, since the graves of Rob, his wife and two of his sons are pointed out here, but the stones which mark them date from long before Rob Roy's time.

And then there's Aberfoyle, where Frank Osbaldistone and Bailie Nicol Jarvie, in the novel, arrive in search of the Bailie's distant relative Rob Roy. None of this has anything to do with the historical Rob, and neither do the inns, trees and plough coulters displayed for the tourist's delight, since Frank and the Bailie existed only in the fertile imagination of Walter Scott. The Highland outlaw was just the figure Scott required for his exploration of the idea of the romantic Highlands, which attracted him as a man and a novelist even while, as an Edinburgh lawyer, he could see its fatal flaws. The douce Glasgow merchant Bailie Nicol Jarvie acquits himself well in his Aberfoyle adventures, but finds that he's not really cut out for the outlaw life:

> I wadna gie the finest sight we hae seen in the Hielands for the first keek o' the
> Gorbals o' Glasgow; and if I were ance there, it suldna be every fule's errand,
> begging your pardon, Mr Francis, that suld take me out o' sight o' Saint Mungo's
> steeple again!

Even today, though, we can see that the Trossachs, all mountains and lochs and wooded glens, is the very sort of landscape in which an outlaw might thrive. The same applies, on a larger scale, to the wide country west of the Great Glen where Bonnie Prince Charlie wandered as a fugitive after the battle of Culloden, ranging much farther than Rob Roy ever did. He made first for the Western Isles, hoping to find a ship which would take him to France. There he spent the long light months of May and June, sleeping sometimes in caves, sometimes in the comparative comfort of huts or cottages. (His route has been carefully pieced together from contemporary accounts and traditions, so that we can see the caves and houses, or at least their sites or ruins.) In South Uist, as everyone knows, he met Flora MacDonald, and travelled with her for several days, awkwardly disguised in skirts and petticoats as her Irish maid Betty Burke, and making that short yet epic journey 'over the sea to Skye'.

From Skye he crossed back to the mainland, and spent the rest of the summer doubling to and fro through the glens to evade the searching soldiers. The Highland weather was not always agreeable, and the food and

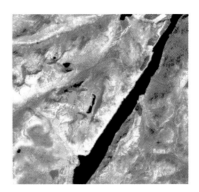

beds sometimes fell short of princely standards, though there was an excellent cave in the Braes of Glenmoriston where he was 'as comfortably lodged as if he had been in a royal palace'. After a while Charles seems to have coped quite well. Towards the end of his wanderings a messenger found that he wasn't in the expected hiding-place, but up the hill with his gun. When he came down the visitor reported on his state:

> . . . barefooted, an old black kilt coat on, philabeg and waistcoat, a dirty shirt
> and a long red beard, a gun in his hand, a pistol and dirk by his side. He was
> very cheerful and in good health, and in my opinion fatter than when he was
> in Inverness.

Not long after that he came to Cluny's Cage on Ben Alder, above Loch Ericht. The famous refuge of the clan chief Cluny Macpherson was a fairly commodious one (half-a-dozen fugitives were already there when Charles and his party arrived), being a two-storey hut built into the mountainside, screened by a thicket of holly and with a good view of anyone who might approach. A cooking-fire could safely be lit, it had been found, because against the grey rock face the trickle of smoke wouldn't be seen. It was a hiding-place fit for a prince.

So it must have seemed to Robert Louis Stevenson over a hundred years later, when, for the purposes of his novel *Kidnapped*, two more fugitives had to take to the heather. The trouble begins for David Balfour when he accidentally witnesses the Appin Murder. This is a historical incident and the assassin has never been officially identified. The name, so it's said, has been handed down by those in the secret – ''Tis known in Appin' – and has in fact been revealed by more than one modern writer, though unfortunately it's not always the same name which is unveiled. Most writers assure us that it wasn't Alan Breck Stewart, but Stevenson keeps us guessing for a time. (As well as being a romantic fictional character in *Kidnapped*, Alan Breck does feature in accounts of the real-life killing.)

In the novel, David finds Alan Breck in slightly suspicious circumstances, on the hillside above the murder scene, 'just inside the shelter of the trees':

> He gave me no salutation; indeed it was no time for civilities; only 'Come!' says he,
> and set off running along the side of the mountain towards Ballachulish; and I,
> like a sheep, to follow him.

They're on the run because, even if Alan isn't the killer, David unfortunately chanced to speak to the victim just before the fatal shot rang out, and so is being hunted as an accomplice. They have to get out of the Highlands into the civilised Lowlands, where David has friends and, just as important, a lawyer. Their route, like that

of Bonnie Prince Charlie, has been diligently researched and walked by many enthusiasts. It may be that R. L. S. himself hadn't walked it, because he makes them leap a waterfall in Glencoe when it would have been far easier to ford a burn. (Though the leap is more dramatic, and this is fiction after all.)

In Glencoe they spend a long hot day hiding on top of a rock (also placed there by Stevenson, it appears, when there wasn't a suitable one to hand) and then it's over Rannoch Moor, pursued by cavalry riding at most unlikely speed for the rough terrain, to Ben Alder and Cluny's Cage. Cluny Macpherson is in residence, still a fugitive, for the setting date of *Kidnapped* is not long after 1745–6, Bliadhna Tearlaich or Charlie's Year. R. L. S. knows the Prince's story, and his imagination fills in the details of this idyllic place:

> The trunks of several trees had been wattled across, the intervals strengthened
> with stakes, and the ground behind this barricade levelled up with earth to make
> the floor. A tree, which grew out from the hillside, was the living centre-beam of
> the roof. The walls were of wattle and covered with moss. The whole house had
> something of an egg shape; and it half hung, half stood in that steep, hillside
> thicket, like a wasps' nest in a green hawthorn.

But David's stay there is not happy. He comes down with a fever, and still isn't well when they take up their journey again, which leads to a miserable quarrel with Alan. He finds shelter in a friendly house in Balquhidder, and there he is visited by Robin Oig, 'one of the sons of the notorious Rob Roy'. As we have remarked, in this countryside you can't get away from Rob Roy.

Neil Munro as a historical novelist is often overshadowed by R. L. S., but *John Splendid* is worth reading in its own right. Again there's a painful journey at the heart of the book. In fact there are two, for young Elrigmore and his older companion John McIver, 'John Splendid', are captured on a scouting expedition and taken along on what became known as Montrose's Miraculous Journey to Inverlochy. This was a forced march through the mountains at the end of January, and by tradition it took just two days. That was the miracle, given the weather they travelled through:

> The pass of Corryarick met us with a girning face and white fangs . . . The drifts
> lay waist high, the horses plunged to the belly-bands, the foot-men pushed
> through in a sweat . . . We were lost in a wilderness of mountain-peaks; the bens
> started about us on every hand like the horrors of a nightmare, every ben with its
> death-sheet, menacing us, poor insects, crawling in our pain across the landscape.

The battle of Inverlochy is a disaster for their chieftain MacCailein Mor, the Marquis of Argyll, and the prisoners are allowed to go home. With an ill-assorted group of companions, they are 'seven broken men' in a desperate plight, because they are in enemy country: 'the sight of our tartan in any one of [these] glens would rouse hell in every heart about us'.

When they reach the house of Dalness in Glen Etive, however, things seem to be looking up. The house is lit from end to end, with blazing hearth-fires and laden supper-tables. Weary and starving, they can't resist the chance of shelter and food, particularly since there isn't a soul to be seen. Of course, it's a trap, and the fugitives have a long way to go yet before they reach 'the highway of Loch Finne that leads down the slope of the sea' to Inveraray, where Neil Munro was brought up and where most of his books find themselves at home.

John Buchan's childhood country creeps into his books too. He admired both Stevenson and Munro, but his best-known adventure stories have a contemporary setting, and his fugitives, like Richard Hannay in *The Thirty-Nine Steps*, have to contend not with horse-soldiers but with a more up-to-date form of pursuit. Hannay is 'on the central boss of a huge upland country', in fact the Galloway moors. He can see everything for miles around, but, unfortunately, everything can see him: 'There was no cover for a tomtit in those bald green places . . . Then I saw an aeroplane coming up from the east.'

But hi-tech surveillance methods can go only so far. Soon it's man against man, the pursuers on the hillside below beating the heather, while Hannay takes an equally traditional route:

> I crawled out of my shelf into the cover of a boulder, and from it gained a shallow trench which slanted up the mountain face. This led me presently into the narrow gully of a burn, by way of which I scrambled to the top of the ridge . . . I pretended to retreat over the skyline, but instead went back the way I had come, and in twenty minutes was behind the ridge overlooking my sleeping place. From that viewpoint I had the satisfaction of seeing the pursuit streaming up the hill at the top of the glen on a hopelessly false scent.

Just like Rob Roy, and the Prince, and David Balfour, the fugitive is off into the heather, making full use of the hills and burns and glens, and the landscape of Scotland, once again, is playing its part in the story.

17 Between Worlds

For Kilmeny had been she knew not where,
And Kilmeny had seen what she could not declare;
Kilmeny had been where the cock never crew,
Where the rain never fell, and the wind never blew . . .

James Hogg

There are so many ways to experience the landscape. There's the scientific route, through geology for instance, learning how the mountains and the lochs came to be where they are. Then history lends its shading to the picture: we see Glencoe in a shroud of foreboding because of the massacre, and Iona in a heavenly light because we know about Columba. After that, legend and poetry come in. The Borders historian John Veitch sums it up in a phrase, writing about the famously poetical Yarrow valley: 'The Yarrow we now feel is not altogether the Yarrow we see.'

And the landscape that we feel can sometimes, to a sensitive observer, give a hint of what may be there. Lewis Spence imagines such a place:

> The muir is mirk, yet no wi' nicht,
> The muir is bricht, but no wi' day,
> But be it nicht or be it licht
> Is nocht to the fouk o Harmisay.
>
> For theirs is a dowfer nicht than nicht,
> An' theirs is a glintler day than day;
> They hae the glaik that glamours the sicht,
> The fouk o the clachan o Harmisay . . .

In Loch Voshimid on Harris there's a small island which had that sort of effect on J. M. Barrie, when he spent a holiday nearby. He also heard a local story of a girl who was taken away by the fairies. According to the tradition – which is found in many cultures – she came back believing that no time had passed, only to discover that everyone she knew had grown old. From such roots grew Barrie's play *Mary Rose* with its spooky 'island that likes to be visited':

> There seemed to us to be nothing very particular about the island, unless, perhaps,
> that it is curiously complete in itself. There is a tiny pool in it that might be called
> a lake, out of which a stream flows. It has hillocks and a glade, a sort of miniature
> land. That was all we noticed, though it became the most dreaded place in the
> world to us.

Behind the landscape that we see there's that other, stranger landscape, and some people are at home in it. James Hogg's grandfather, Will Laidlaw of Phaup, whose gravestone is to be seen in Ettrick kirkyard beside Hogg's, was famous as having been the last man in that countryside to see and talk with the fairies. But 'fairies'

is a kind of catch-all term which poses more questions than it answers: if Will o' Phaup did see the inhabitants of another world, who were they, and where did they come from?

Some of them, it's always been thought, might be the spirits of the dead, waiting for some unfinished business to be settled before they can go: a murder to be avenged, a name supplied for an unbaptised child. Alternatively, they might be the old gods or nature spirits, supplanted by Christianity but still in attendance on their holy wells and standing stones. There's another tempting theory that they are a folk memory of real people who used to be here. Fairy hills, so called in tradition, often turn out to be ancient burial mounds, just as the stones known as 'elf-arrows' are prehistoric flint arrowheads. The small underground dwellers in the fairy hills may have been the early inhabitants driven into hiding by successive waves of invaders. James Hogg brought this idea nearer to his own time in his story 'The Brownie of Bodsbeck', with fugitive Covenanters singing and praying in the wild Borders hills:

> These hymns . . . were often heard at a great distance, causing no little consternation to the remote dwellers of that mountain region. The heart of the shepherd grew chill, and his hairs stood on end, as he hasted home to alarm the cottage circle with a tale of horror. For, besides this solemn and unearthly music, he perceived lights moving about by night . . . and he deemed that legions of spiritual creatures had once more taken possession of his solitary dells.

But these are explanations thought up in comparatively recent years. Better, previous generations have felt, not to try to explain what shouldn't be explained. Better to accept and accommodate these people, who have always been there.

So wherever you look in the Scottish landscape there are half-seen forms, sometimes grim hags, sometimes handsome men or beautiful maidens whose malevolence is discovered too late. They may be in animal shape, like the kelpie or the fearsome water-bull. There are also fairy sea-cattle who are pleasanter to deal with, and whose bulls may mate with mortal cows, much improving the farmer's stock. Too bad if, like one Hebridean crofter, you get rid of all the mortal calves and keep only the fairy stock, only to find that one day they all make for the shore and disappear under the waves.

That's not to mention the apparently real creatures who may have their own agenda:

As I was walking all alane
I heard twa corbies making a mane;
The tane unto the t'other say,
'Where sall we gang and dine today?'

'In behint yon auld fail dyke,
I wot there lies a new-slain knight;
And naebody kens that he lies there
But his hawk, his hound, and his lady fair . . .

Ye'll sit on his white hause-bane,
And I'll pike out his bonny blue een;
Wi' ae lock o' his gowden hair
We'll theek our nest when it grows bare.'

Andrew Greig uses this haunting image to great effect in his novel *When They Lay Bare*. A set of plates painted with the scenes of the ballad is the starting-point for a dark, ambiguous story of love and betrayal:

Peer more closely now [at the plates]. That darker green below the dyke, half-hidden among the skeletal bracken, is surely a cape, and there's the hunch of a shoulder and legs folded up to the chin. There is someone behind the wall, and it's not a new-slain knight. It is a woman, waiting. (There is always a woman waiting.)

Sometimes these people, or creatures, are heard, not seen. Ben Dorain in Argyll is famous for the sounds heard there at night: natural or otherwise, who can say? 'There's aye keening on Ben Dorain,' says a Gaelic song. There's keening too in Glencoe, where a *caoineag*, or weeper, constantly laments the massacre. This is the same creature heard in George Campbell Hay's poem 'Three Brothers'. The brothers haven't returned after a voyage and their families can only wait through a long night:

Afore the brekk o day in the moarnin,
when it wasna derk and it wasna dawnin,
from the rocks on the rhu they heard a cryin,
a *ceinteach*'s keenin. They kent ther story.

> They kent what thon sore cry was sayin,
> and whose lair was laid in the wrack and seaweed,
> and they sat there wi the day brekkin,
> grey face on the men and the wummen greetin.

Sometimes you see them and wish you hadn't. Walking on the hills, you may stop to drink at a spring and find a woman washing bloodstained clothes in the clear water, weeping as she works. This is the dreadful bean nighe, the washerwoman, and you should hope that you don't recognise the clothes as yours.

Part of the Minch, the stretch of water between the Outer Hebrides and the mainland, is known as Sruth nam Fear Gorma, the strait of the blue men. The Blue Men operate by swimming out to capsize ships (unless the skipper is alert enough to keep up with them in rhyming games), and they constitute only one of the many hazards of life at sea. It's no wonder that fishing communities had (and still have) a code of superstitions; actions and words that must or must not be done or spoken, to bring luck or, more urgently, avert disaster.

Because who knows what's in the sea? Certainly there are seals, or selkies, which in Orkney and Shetland at least can assume human form and have a long history of interaction with us. There's the seal-woman whose seal-skin, discarded for sunbathing on the rocks, is stolen by a watching islander. He takes it home, and she has to follow and live as his wife, mourning all the time for the lost freedom of the sea. And there's the strong and irresistible seal-man who makes his move on a mortal woman. Eric Linklater uses this legend in his story 'Sealskin Trousers', where the girl's human partner arrives on the scene to find that he has come just too late:

> They began to mock me . . . I heard his voice quite clearly, and honesty compels
> me to admit that it was singularly sweet and the tune was the most haunting I
> have ever heard. They were about forty yards away, two seals swimming together,
> and the evening light was so clear and taut that his voice might have been the
> vibration of an invisible bow across its coloured bands . . .

And what is the seal singing? Why, of course, it's the traditional ballad of the seal-man who fathers a child on a human wife:

> I am a man upo the lan,
> I am a silkie in the sea;
> And when I'm far and far frae lan
> My dwelling is in Sule Skerrie.

As selkies come out of the sea, humans in their turn go into the other world, generally by way of a fairy hill. Orkney is full of 'trow' (or troll) place-names, such as the Trowie Glen in the island of Hoy, and legends like the one of the fiddler who is howe-taken – snatched into the fairy hill – to return years later, unchanged. (That, of course, was the experience of Rip van Winkle, whose American author, Washington Irving, was of Orkney descent.) In the islands you can still hear 'trowie tunes', folk music with no known source, which therefore – perhaps – has been learned from the trows.

It's not at all uncommon, then, for humans to be abducted by fairies who appreciated their music or just like the look of them. The fairies' intention with James Hogg's Kilmeny is show her off to all of fairyland as the epitome of sinless womanhood, but some kidnappers, like the Queen of the Fairies who lured Thomas the Rhymer away, have other purposes in mind. In the ballad of 'Tam Lin' it's a mortal, and a woman, who makes the first move:

> O I forbid you, maidens a'
> That wear gowd on your hair,
> To come or gae by Carterhaugh,
> For young Tam Lin is there . . .
>
> Janet has kilted her green kirtle
> A little aboon her knee,
> And she has broded her yellow hair
> A little aboon her bree,
> And she's awa to Carterhaugh,
> As fast as she can hie.

Before long Janet is with child to the otherworldly Tam Lin. Since she needs an acknowledged father for her bairn, it's fortunate that Tam Lin is himself human, stolen (like the Rhymer) by the susceptible Queen of the Fairies. Janet rescues him by holding fast through all the ordeals the fairies can contrive, as he turns in her arms, successively, into a snake, a lion, a bar of red-hot iron . . . At last he becomes 'a naked knight' and all she has to do is cover him with her green mantle and take him home.

Liz Lochhead has written a very funny feminist deconstruction of this, 'Tam Lin's Lady':

> And if, as the story goes nine times out of ten –
> he took you by the milkwhite hand & by the grassgreen sleeve
> & laid you on the bonnie bank & asked of you no leave,
> well, so what?
> You're not the first to fall for it,
> good green girdle and all . . .

It's as well to take the warning that there could be other explanations for these marvellous events. The Reverend Robert Kirk, minister of Aberfoyle, was spirited away by the fairies as recently as 1692. At least, he was found dead on the fairy hill, and since he was a seventh son, therefore in touch with the other world, the case was held to be proven. (He had also written a book on fairies, *The Secret Commonwealth*, which, it was surmised at the time, might have annoyed these strange folk.)

John Buchan in his novel *Witch Wood* plays on the story of Robert Kirk. His young minister also disappears in mysterious circumstances:

> Sandy Nicoll saw him in the gloaming moving with leaps which were beyond a
> mortal's power across Charlie's Moss. Later . . . he was observed by a drover to cross
> the peat-road, and the drover – his name was Grieve – swore to his dying-day that
> beside the traveller moved a coal-black shadow . . .

We, the readers, are allowed to know the real situation, since the last paragraphs of the novel show us the minister, with a friend, taking ship for Bergen in a perfectly earthly escape from various sorts of trouble. But the legend remains.

Even if you keep away from fairy hills, you can't be entirely safe. There, on the map, or before your eyes, to prove it, is Beinn a'Ghlo, the veiled mountain, on whose misty summit crouches a weather-controlling witch; or Sgriob na Cailleach, a scar on one of the Paps of Jura raked by another witch's broomstick as she flew past. We all know what happened to Tam o' Shanter, and he was only coming home from the pub:

> When, glimmering thro' the groaning trees,
> Kirk-Alloway seem'd in a bleeze;
> Thro' ilka bore the beams were glancing;
> And loud resounded mirth and dancing . . .
> Warlocks and witches in a dance . . .

But the dancing stopped when witchcraft was diagnosed in a neighbourhood and real women were condemned for imaginary crimes. It happened in Orkney, and George Mackay Brown returns more than once in his poetry to the grim hill of Gallowsha above Kirkwall, where 'the hangman put the red shirt' on a bewildered and totally innocent young woman:

> Three horsemen rode between the hills
> And they dismounted at Greenhill.
> Tall they stooped in at the door.
> No long time then
> Till Wilma came out among them, laughing . . .

It happened in Paisley in the late seventeenth century, for a complex of reasons not yet entirely teased out, including perhaps religious rigour and the spite of a teenage girl. The accuser was Christian Shaw, who became a minister's wife and was later the inspiration behind the Paisley thread industry. Naomi Mitchison in her novel *The Bull Calves* puts her heroine Kirstie on the fringes of that story:

> It was my good-sister, it was Christian Shaw of Bargarran, that brought me to the
> knowledge of *them* and their doings. Although I would never have known what
> kind of a thing she was speaking of if it hadna been for the hate and sin in my
> own heart . . . And they tell't me what to do . . . and we made the image of wax
> with the clippings of Andrew's hair in't, and we did what we shouldna do, and he
> grew ill . . .

There were antidotes to these things. In the Western Isles old charms against evil were blended with newer prayers: 'I will go rightways with the sun,' one blessing runs, 'in name of Ariel and the angels nine.' Cold iron, red thread, running water, the rowan tree; these are some of the ways to protect yourself against the threats of the dark night, half-seen or invisible, real or imagined, malicious spirits or unexplained illnesses. If you thought the old man up the hill might be a warlock, the rowan tree at your door would give you strength and keep you safe. But Violet Jacob suggests that what protects you is your belief in its power: 'For the warlock's livin' yet – *But the rowan's deid*!'

The night of Hallowe'en is the interface between this world and the next. It is All Hallows Eve, the night before All Saints Day, but it has taken over from the old Celtic festival of Samhain. The American imports of pumpkins and trick-or-treat have little to do with this night in Scotland, full of darkness and flame and shape-shifting,

as people in disguise go about with shaded lights. The traveller storyteller Duncan Williamson explains how it is 'the night when the Devil gets loose':

> It is his special night of freedom, when he and all the imps leave Hell, come and spread out through all the country . . . At the centre of the Hallowe'en festival, even today, is the idea that the Devil is not to be clearly seen. Children dress up and put on 'false faces' at Hallowe'en just like the pagans did during their festival when the Devil came; he could walk among them and no-one could distinguish him from the rest.

And the devil is a strong presence in Scottish literature. Burns may address him lightly: 'O thou, whatever title suit thee! Auld Hornie, Satan, Nick, or Clootie . . .' and admit that wind-blown reeds or a startled bird can easily frighten the nervous traveller, but there he is in Kirk Alloway playing the pipes for the witches' dance. There he is, grimly, cited in the witch trials, as one poor woman after another confesses to dealings with her Master.

More subtly and more disturbingly, there he is in James Hogg's great novel *The Private Memoirs and Confessions of a Justified Sinner*. He becomes the constant companion of the central character Robert, though strangely enough his appearance is slightly different each time he is seen. 'By looking at a person attentively,' he explains, if you can call it explaining, 'I by degrees assume his likeness, and by assuming his likeness I attain to the possession of his most secret thoughts.'

He is never named as the devil. Is he, in fact, a projection of Robert's own thoughts and desires? In the haunted landscape of Scotland, nothing is quite as it seems.

18 The Skinklan Stars

Mars is braw in crammasy,
Venus in a green silk goun,
The auld mune shaks her gowden feathers
Their starry talk's a wheen o' blethers . . .

Hugh MacDiarmid

Wide skies arch over Scotland, full of great winds, clouds and light. Kathleen Jamie finds more there:

Skeins o geese write a word
across the sky. A word
struck lik a gong
afore I wis born.
The sky moves like cattle, lowin.

Above the flat country of Caithness, as Robin Fulton sees, their beauty takes the breath away:

Sky is larger than life; land is small
Under it; between you and the square edge of Hoy
Atlantic toilers shoulder through the Firth
As blue and white as in a Book of Hours:
It is almost as clear as on God's fifth day.

Equally, when it's dark, there's a lot of sky out there. The Celtic people measured their year by light. As the Christian church year now begins at the end of November with Advent, so the pagan year began in darkness, at Samhain, now Hallowe'en. The light grows with the lengthening days, until, in the Celtic calendar, the bonfires of Beltane, the first of May, greet the time of full light.

It's possible that prehistoric stone circles like Callanish in Lewis and the Ring of Brodgar in Orkney were deliberately aligned in relation to the position of the sun and moon at significant times of the year. The question is fiercely debated, but what is certain – you can even buy a postcard to prove it – is the strange and beautiful sight to be seen at sunset, weather permitting, on Midwinter Day inside Maeshowe, the great chambered tomb not far from Brodgar. George Mackay Brown saw it:

The winter sun hangs just over the ridge of the Coolags. Its setting will seal the shortest day of the year, the winter solstice . . . Stoop through the long narrow corridor towards the chamber of darkness, winter, death. Now the hills of Hoy – strangely similar in shape to Maeshowe – are about to take the dying sun and huddle it away. The sun sends out a few last weak beams.

One of the light rays is caught in this stone web of death. Through the long
corridor it has found its way; it splashes the far wall of the chamber. (In five
or six thousand years there has been, one assumes, a slight wobble in the earth's
axis; originally, on that first solstice, the last of the sun would have struck directly
on the tomb where possibly the king-priest was lying with all his grave-goods
around him . . .)

The illumination lasts for a few minutes, then is quenched. It is a brief fleeting
thing; yet it is a seal on the dying year, a pledge of renewal, a cry of resurrection.

F. Marian McNeill remarks practically that primitive man was a realist: 'If he worshipped the sun and the moon
and the heavenly bodies, it was not primarily for their inherent mystery . . . but because they mysteriously
regulated the seasons and brought him food.' He has left us many signs that at least he greatly respected the
sun. Not just rites and processions but everyday movements – walking round a house or church, launching
a boat – had to be carried out clockwise, as the sun moves. In Barra, we're told, men used to take off their
bonnets to the sun, and there are sun poems in *Carmina Gadelica*:

> Glòir dhuit fhèin,
> A ghrèin an àigh.
> Glòir dhuit fhèin, a ghrèin,
> A ghnùis Dhè nan dùl.
>
> Glory to thee,
> Thou glorious sun,
> Glory to thee, thou sun,
> Face of the God of life!

And while men acknowledged the sun, women in Barra used to bow to the moon, greeting her as we still
sometimes do today:

> Fàilte dhut, a ghealach ùr,
> Àilleagan iùil na bàidh!
> Ta mi lùbadh dhut mo ghlùn,
> Ta mi cùrnadh dhut mo ghràidh . . .

A rìoghainn an iùil,
A rìoghainn an àigh,
A rìoghainn mo rùin,
A ghealach ùr nan tràth!

Hail to thee, new moon,
Guiding jewel of gentleness!
I am bending to thee my knee,
I am offering thee my love . . .

Thou queen-maiden of guidance,
Thou queen-maiden of good fortune,
Thou queen-maiden my beloved,
Thou new moon of the seasons!

But in some cultures the moon was too sacred, or too powerful, to name. Shetland fishermen used the tabu-name 'Glunta' instead, and Robert Alan Jamieson voices their prayer:

Glunta, owre aa,
Be under Ert,
Mak fast wir motion,
Turn daeth.

Glunta, cover aa,
Be owre Ert,
Mak fast wir motion,
Weigh life.

In the Highlands, as elsewhere, the full moon after the autumn equinox is the harvest moon or Michaelmas moon. Neil Munro quotes the saying that the Highlanders of Lochaber 'pay their daughters' tochers by the light of the Michaelmas moon', because this was the high season for cattle-rustling, when the cattle were in prime condition for market and the night nearly as bright as day. Next, in October, comes the hunters' moon, which is also known as the badgers' moon, because the badger prepares energetically for winter, as everyone (it was reckoned) ought to do. And Edwin Morgan sees a stranger beauty in a city Guy Fawkes moon:

Fog shroud
and clouds
(when the clock
chimed late
in the heavy
November night-
time) lifting
the mystery
for a greater
drifted
off a whole
white full
moon pitched
above the white
thin chimney-
stalk of the
new Dawsholm
incinerator . . .

The three most beautiful things in the world, so it's said in the islands, are a full moon, a full-rigged ship, and a woman with child. But, in spite of the beauty and the mystery, moonlight is a melancholy light. William Soutar captures the essential loneliness of the wandering moon:

Saftly, saftly, throu the mirk,
the mune walks aa hersel:
ayont the brae; abune the kirk;
and owre the dunnlan bell.
I wadna be the mune at nicht
for aa her gowd and aa her licht.

Robert Louis Stevenson considered nostalgically, in adulthood, that 'there are no stars so lovely as Edinburgh street-lamps'. Because of light pollution, city dwellers today don't get the full effect of a starry sky, but young Louis as a child was able to see not the street-lamps but the stars themselves:

The Dog, and the Plough, and the Hunter, and all,
And the star of the sailor, and Mars,
These shone in the sky, and the pail by the wall
Would be half full of water and stars.

And over Hoy Sound in Orkney – one of the places where the glory can still be seen – there's a star-filled sky
for George Mackay Brown's lobster fisherman to contemplate, along with a star that shone two millennia ago:

Tae be wan o them Kings
That owre the desert rode
Trackan a muckle reid star,
The herald o God!

Tae swivel a crystal eye
Abune a mountain place
And light on an uncan star,
A tinker in space! –

Thought Tammas, rowan his boat
Fae creel tae creel aroond,
When Venus shook her hair
Owre the Soond.

Sorley MacLean sees something even more remote:

Lìonmhoireachd anns na speuran,
òr-chriathair muillionan de reultan,
fuar, fad as, lòghmhor, àlainn,
tosdach, neo-fhaireachdail, neo-fhàilteach.

Lànachd an eòlais m' an cùrsa,
failmhe an aineolais gun iùl-chairt,
cruinne-cé ag gluasad sàmhach,
aigne leis fhéin anns an àruinn.

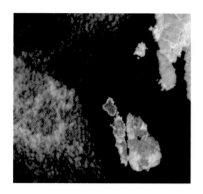

Multitude of the skies,
golden riddle of millions of stars,
cold distant lustrous beautiful,
silent, unfeeling, unwelcoming.

Fullness of knowledge in their course
emptiness of chartless ignorance,
a universe moving in silence,
a mind alone in its bounds.

And when Hugh MacDiarmid looked up into the Langholm night, he saw more than was actually visible. One of his famous early poems begins:

I' the how-dumb-deid o' the cauld hairst nicht
The warl' like an eemis stane
Wags i' the lift . . .

An eemis stane is a logan-stone, a huge boulder naturally balanced on another so delicately that a touch will set it rocking. It's a brilliant image of the earth in its orbit round the sun, tilting, as we know it does, to and fro. We can see it quite clearly in the mind's eye, but then we've seen the pictures taken on the Apollo missions. When MacDiarmid conceived the poem it was only his powerful imagination which could envisage the blue earth in the black sky, so strangely familiar to us now.

Edwin Morgan, a generation younger than MacDiarmid, has seen those Apollo pictures and assimilated them in his work. He is the poet of space, whether he is dealing with men visiting another planet or aliens discovering earth. In his poems the last doomed earthlings, living in caves, still remember a few words from their old life: '. . . we went out in fireflauchts and gnashings of teeth . . .' He can even speak in the voice of the lunar module which carried Armstrong and Aldrin to their landing in the Sea of Tranquillity:

It is black so. There is that dust.
My ladder in light. What are my men . . .
Sharp is a shadow. A horizon goes flat.
All rock are samples. Dust taken I think . . .
That moon is here. They have some dust.
Is home they know. Blue earth I think . . .

Much has changed in the last few years since Iain M. Banks began to document his futuristic civilisation, the Culture, in *Consider Phlebas*, the first of the science fiction novels which he has published alternately with the straight novels he writes as plain Iain Banks. Novelists like Ken MacLeod, whose *The Stone Canal* is set on a distant planet but has connections with mid-twentieth century Glasgow, and Paul Johnston, whose crime novels take place in a sinister future Edinburgh, are bringing science fiction into the mainstream of Scottish writing. Ahead of them, as so often, was Naomi Mitchison, whose *Memoirs of a Spacewoman* was first published in 1962. Her character Mary is no alien but a real woman – an earthwoman, a Terran – with experiences we recognise, and some we don't:

> One is told about time blackout. It was my mother who told me. She was just back
> from a voyage, and I had suddenly realised that, although I had been growing up
> and feeling in every cell of my body the marvellous beautiful sweep of the Terran
> seasons, the Arctic spring, the flickering lightning of the monsoons, the crash of
> the west Atlantic hurricanes, yet she seemed unchanged.

So the landscape of Scottish writing stretches beyond the mountains and glens, the past and present, to another place and time. The young poet Colin Donati brings together science and history and architecture and literature in one wide sweep:

> If ae rock conjures Scotland up for me
> It isna Cairngorm quartz, sclenters, scree,
> Sanct Giles croon, brig-uphaudin key,
> Croon's jasp, cross or 'stane o destinie';
> nor is it dyke or broch, nor stack nor dun,
> nae fog-coored, rune-scrart, eemis i' the sun
> raised beach or sicna prentit fossilry,
> Fingal's basalt, pap o' Bennachie,
> hud, cairn, whun, sheel, elf-cup, putt or skerry
> the rock that conjures Scotland up for me
> gies licht in aatum, shines for aa to see
> an is the hairst Mune, heich an far an wee.

His vision encompasses the space age into which he was born, and all the ages of Scotland, back to the rocks with which this book began: today and yesterday, and, you can't doubt it, tomorrow.

Bibliography

This is a very selective bibliography listing some of the Scottish writers and works quoted or mentioned in *Land Lines*. (Other work by these authors may be found in the anthologies listed below.) To help place the writers in the broad landscape of Scottish literature, the original date of publication is given in square brackets for older titles, followed by a modern edition if there is one.

Aboulela, Leila, *The Translator*, Edinburgh: Polygon, 1999.

Banks, Iain, *The Bridge*, London: Macmillan, 1986.

— *The Crow Road*, London: Scribners, 1992.

— [as Iain M. Banks] *Consider Phlebas*, London: Macmillan, 1987.

Barrie, J. M., *Auld Licht Idylls* [1888].

— *Mary Rose* [1924], Oxford: Oxford University Press, 1995 [with *Peter Pan*].

— *Farewell Miss Julie Logan* [1932], Edinburgh: Canongate, 2000.

Blake, George, *The Shipbuilders* [1935], Edinburgh: B & W Publishing,1993.

Boswell, James, *The Journal of a Tour to the Hebrides* [1785], London: Penguin, 1984

— [with Samuel Johnson] *A Journey to the Western Islands of Scotland* [1785], London: Penguin, 1984.

Brooksbank, Mary, *Sidlaw Breezes* [1966], Dundee: David Winter, 1982.

Brown, George Douglas, *The House with the Green Shutters* [1901], London: Penguin, 1985.

Brown, George Mackay, *Poems New and Selected*, London: Hogarth Press, 1971.

— *Under Brinkie's Brae* [essays], Edinburgh: Gordon Wright, 1979.

— *Selected Poems 1954–83*, London: John Murray, 1991.

Buchan, John, *The Thirty-Nine Steps* [1915], London: Penguin, 1956.

— *Witch Wood* [1927], Edinburgh: Canongate, 1988.

— *Poems Scots and English*, Edinburgh: Thomas Nelson, 1953.

Burgess, J. J. Haldane, *Rasmie's Buddie* [c. 1900], Lerwick: Shetland Publishing Company, 1979.

Burns, Robert, *Poems and Songs* [1786–91], Oxford: Oxford University Press, 1969.

Burnside, John, *The Asylum Dance*, London: Jonathan Cape, 2000.

Campbell, Thomas, *Poetical Works* [1854].

Carmichael, Alexander, *Carmina Gadelica* [1900–71], Edinburgh: Floris Books, 1992.

Corrie, Joe, *The Image o' God and other poems*, [1937].

Cruickshank, Helen B., *Collected Poems*, Edinburgh: Reprographia, 1971.

Davidson, John, *The Poems of John Davidson* [1890–1905], Aberdeen: Association for Scottish Literary Studies, 1973.

Donati, Colin, *A forest seen through the belly of a dinosaur*, Edinburgh: School of Poets, 1997.

Drinan, Adam, *The Ghosts of the Strath* [1943].

Dunbar, William, *The Poems of William Dunbar* [15th–16th century], Aberdeen: Association for Scottish Literary Studies, 1998.

Dunn, Douglas, *Selected Poems* 1964-83, London: Faber and Faber, 1986.

Dutton, G. F., *Squaring the Waves*, Newcastle: Bloodaxe Books, 1986.

Fergusson, Robert, *Selected Poems* [1773], Edinburgh: Birlinn, 2000.

Finlay, Ian Hamilton, *The Dancers Inherit the Party* [1960], Edinburgh: Polygon, 1996.

Fraser, G. S., *Poems*, Leicester: Leicester University Press, 1981.

Fraser, Olive, *The Wrong Music: the poems of Olive Fraser 1909–1977*, Edinburgh: Canongate, 1989.

Fulton, Robin, *Selected Poems*, Edinburgh: Macdonald, 1980.

Galt, John, *Annals of the Parish* [1821], Edinburgh: Mercat Press, 1983.

— *The Entail* [1823].

Garioch, Robert, *Complete Poetical Works*, Edinburgh: Macdonald, 1983.

Garry, Flora, *Collected Poems*, Edinburgh: Gordon Wright Publishing, 1995.

Gibbon, Lewis Grassic, *Sunset Song* [1932], Edinburgh: Canongate, 1988.

— *A Scots Hairst* [short stories and essays], ed. I. S. Munro, Hutchinson, 1967.

Gorman, Rody, *Air a' Charbad fo Thalamh/On the Underground*, Edinburgh: Polygon, 2000.

Grant, Elizabeth, *Memoirs of a Highland Lady* [1898], Edinburgh: Canongate, 1988.

Gray, Alasdair, *Lanark*, Edinburgh: Canongate, 1981.

Gray, Alexander, *Selected Poems*, Glasgow: William MacLellan, 1948.

Greig, Andrew, *When They Lay Bare*, London: Faber and Faber, 1999.

Gunn, Neil, *Butcher's Broom* [1934], London: Souvenir Press, 1977.

— *Highland River* [1937], Edinburgh: Canongate, 1991.

— *Off in a Boat* [1938], Colonsay: House of Lochar, 1998.

— *The Silver Darlings* [1941], London: Faber and Faber, 1969.

— *The Green Isle of the Great Deep* [1944], London: Souvenir Press, 1975.

— *Landscape and Light* [essays], ed. A. McCleery, Aberdeen: Aberdeen University Press, 1987.

Hamilton, Janet, *Poems and Ballads* [1868].

Hay, George Campbell (Deorsa Mac Iain Deorsa), *Collected Poems and Songs*, Edinburgh: Edinburgh University Press, 2000.

Hay, John MacDougall, *Gillespie* [1914], Edinburgh: Canongate, 1983.

Herbert, W. N., *Cabaret McGonagall*, Newcastle: Bloodaxe Books, 1996.

Hind, Archie, *The Dear Green Place* [1966].

Hogg, James, *Highland Tours* [1802–4], Hawick: Byway Books, 1981.

— *Selected Poems and Songs* [1822], Edinburgh: Scottish Academic Press, 1986.

— *The Private Memoirs and Confessions of a Justified Sinner* [1824], London: Penguin, 1983.

Jacob, Violet, *The Scottish Poems of Violet Jacob*, Edinburgh: Oliver and Boyd, 1944.

Jamie, Kathleen, *The Queen of Sheba*, Newcastle: Bloodaxe Books, 1994.

Jamieson, Robert Alan, *Shoormal*, Edinburgh: Polygon, 1986.

— *Thin Wealth*, Edinburgh: Polygon, 1986.

Johnston, Ellen, *Autobiography, Poems and Songs* [1867].

Johnston, Paul, *Body Politic*, London: Hodder and Stoughton, 1997.

Kelman, James, *How Late it Was, How Late*, London: Secker and Warburg, 1994.

Kennedy, A. L., *Night Geometry and the Garscadden Trains*, Edinburgh: Polygon, 1990.

Kesson, Jessie, *Glitter of Mica* [1963], Edinburgh: Paul Harris, 1982.

— *Somewhere Beyond*, ed. I. Murray, Edinburgh: B & W Publishing, 2000.

Leonard, Tom, *Intimate Voices: selected work 1965–1983*, Newcastle: Galloping Dog Press, 1984.

Linklater, Eric, *The Goose Girl and other stories* [1935–57], Edinburgh: Canongate, 1991.

Livingstone, William (Uilleam MacDhunleibhe), *Duain agus Orain* [1882].

Lochhead, Liz, *Dreaming Frankenstein*, Edinburgh: Polygon, 1984.

Lyndsay, Sir David, *Ane Satyre of the Thrie Estaitis* [1552], Edinburgh: Canongate, 1989.

McArthur, Alexander, *No Mean City* [1935], London: Corgi, 1957.

MacCaig, Norman, *Collected Poems*, London: Chatto and Windus, 1990.

MacColla, Fionn, *And the Cock Crew* [1945], Edinburgh: Canongate, 1995.

McCrone, Guy, *Wax Fruit* [1947], Edinburgh: B & W Publishing, 1993.

MacDiarmid, Hugh, *Complete Poems*, Manchester: Carcanet, 1993.

MacDonald, Alexander (Alasdair MacMhaighstir Alasdair), *The Poems of Alexander MacDonald* [18th century], 1924.

Macfarlan, James, *City Songs* [1855].

MacGill, Patrick, *Children of the Dead End* [1914], Horsham: Caliban, 1982.

McGonagall, William, *Poetic Gems* [1890], Edinburgh: Birlinn, 1992.

McGrath, John, *The Cheviot, the Stag, and the Black, Black Oil* [1974], London: Eyre Methuen, 1981.

McIlvanney, William, *The Kiln*, London: Hodder and Stoughton, 1996.

Macintyre, Duncan (Donnchadh Ban Mac an t-Saoir), *Ben Dorain* [18th century], tr. Iain Crichton Smith, Preston: Akros, 1969.

Mackenzie, Compton, *Whisky Galore* [1947], London: Penguin, 1957.

Maclaren, Ian, *Beside the Bonnie Brier Bush* [1894].

McLean, Duncan, *Blackden*, London: Secker and Warburg, 1994.

MacLean, Sorley (Somerled MacGill-Eain), *O Choille gu Bearradh/From Wood to Ridge*, Manchester: Carcanet, 1989.

McLellan, Robert, *Linmill Stories* [1960–65], Edinburgh: Canongate, 1990.

— *Sweet Largie Bay and Arran Burn*, Preston: Akros, 1977.

MacLeod, Ken, *The Stone Canal*, London: Legend, 1996.

MacNeacail, Aonghas, *An seachnadh/The avoiding*, Edinburgh: Macdonald, 1986.

Macpherson, Mary (Màiri Mhòr nan Oran), [Poems 1891], *Màiri Mhòr nan Oran*, ed. D. Meek, Glasgow: Gairm, 1977.

Martin, Angus, *The Larch Plantation*, Edinburgh: Macdonald, 1990.

Miller, Hugh, *Scenes and Legends of the North of Scotland* [1835], Edinburgh: B & W Publishing, 1994.

Mitchison, Naomi, *The Bull Calves* [1947], Edinburgh: Canongate, 1990.

— *Men and Herring*, Edinburgh: Serif Books, 1949.

— *The Big House* [1950], Edinburgh: Canongate, 1987.

— *Lobsters on the Agenda* [1952], Colonsay: House of Lochar, 1998.

— *Five Men and a Swan*, London: Allen and Unwin, 1957.

— *Memoirs of a Spacewoman* [1962], London: Women's Press, 1985.

— *The Cleansing of the Knife* [poems], Edinburgh: Canongate, 1978.

— *Among You Taking Notes* [autobiography], London: Gollancz, 1985.

— *A Girl Must Live*, Edinburgh: Richard Drew, 1990.

Moon, Lorna, *Doorways in Drumorty* [1926], Aberdeen: Gourdas House, 1981.

Morgan, Edwin, *Collected Poems*, Manchester: Carcanet, 1990.

— *The Maker on High*, Glasgow: Mariscat Press, 1997.

Muir, Edwin, *Scottish Journey* [1935], Edinburgh: Mainstream, 1979.

— *An Autobiography* [1954], Edinburgh: Canongate, 1993.

— *Complete Poems*, Aberdeen: Association for Scottish Literary Studies, 1991.

Munro, Neil, *John Splendid* [1898], Edinburgh: B & W Publishing, 1994.

— *Para Handy* [1906–23], Edinburgh: Birlinn, 1992.

— *The Daft Days* [1907], Edinburgh: Blackwood, 1924.

— *The New Road* [1914], Edinburgh: B & W Publishing, 1994.

— *The Poetry of Neil Munro*, Edinburgh: Blackwood, 1931.

Murray, Charles, *Hamewith: Complete Poems*, Aberdeen: Aberdeen University Press, 1979.

Neill, William, *Wild Places*, Edinburgh: Luath Press, 1985.

Oliphant, Carolina, Lady Nairne, [18th–19th century], *The Life and Songs of the Baroness Nairne* [1869].

Orkneyinga Saga [13th century], tr. H. Palsson and P. Edwards, London: Penguin, 1981.

O'Rourke, Donny, *The Waistband and other poems*, Edinburgh: Polygon, 1997.

Paterson, Don, *Nil Nil*, London: Faber and Faber, 1993.

Rafferty, Sean, *Collected Poems*, Manchester: Carcanet, 1995.

Ramsay, Allan, *The Works of Allan Ramsay* [1721–5], Edinburgh: Scottish Text Society, 1945–74.

Rankin, Ian, *Black and Blue*, London: Orion, 1997.

— *Set in Darkness*, London: Orion, 2000.

Rendall, Robert, *An Island Shore* [poetry and prose], ed. N. Dickson, Kirkwall: Orkney Press, 1990.

Robertson, T. A. ('Vagaland'), *Collected Poems of Vagaland*, Lerwick: Shetland Times, 1975.

Scott, Alexander, *Complete Poems*, Edinburgh: Mercat Press, 1994.

Scott, Andrew Murray, *Estuary Blue*, Edinburgh: Polygon, 2001.

Scott, Tom, *Collected shorter poems of Tom Scott*, Edinburgh: Chapman, 1993.

Scott, Sir Walter, *Collected Poems* [c. 1800–15].

— *Rob Roy* [1818], London: Penguin, 1995.

— *The Voyage of the Pharos* [1837–8], Hamilton: Scottish Library Association, 1998.

Shepherd, Nan, *The Living Mountain* [1977], Edinburgh: Canongate, 1996 [in *The Grampian Quartet*]

Smith, Alexander, *City Poems* [1857].

Smith, Iain Crichton, *Consider the Lilies* [1968], Edinburgh: Canongate, 1997.

— *Collected Poems*, Manchester: Carcanet, 1992.

Smith, Sydney Goodsir, *Collected Poems*, London: John Calder, 1975.

Smollett, Tobias, *The Expedition of Humphry Clinker* [1771], London: Penguin, 1967.

Soutar, William, *Poems of William Soutar* [1933–43], Edinburgh: Scottish Academic Press, 1988.

Spark, Muriel, *The Prime of Miss Jean Brodie* [1961], London: Penguin, 1965.

Spence, Lewis, *Plumes of Time* [1926].

Stevenson, Robert Louis, *Edinburgh: Picturesque Notes* [1879], New York: Barnes & Noble, 1993.

— *Collected Poems* [c. 1880–90].

— *Kidnapped* [1885], London: Penguin, 1994.

— *A Child's Garden of Verses* [1885], London: Puffin, 1952.

— *The Strange Case of Dr Jekyll and Mr Hyde* [1886], London: Penguin, 1979.

Tannahill, Robert, *Poems and Songs* [1815].

Thomson, Derick (Ruaridh MacThomais), *Creachadh na Clarsaich/Plundering the Harp*, Edinburgh: Macdonald, 1982.

— *Smeur an Dochais/Bramble of Hope*, Edinburgh: Canongate, 1991.

Torrington, Jeff, *Swing Hammer Swing!*, London: Secker and Warburg, 1992.

— *The Devil's Carousel*, London: Secker and Warburg, 1996.

Toulmin, David, *Collected Short Stories*, Edinburgh: Gordon Wright, 1992.

Trocchi, Alexander, *Young Adam*, London: John Calder, 1983.

Warner, Alan, *Morvern Callar*, London: Jonathan Cape, 1994.

— *The Sopranos*, London: Jonathan Cape, 1998.

Welsh, Irvine, *Trainspotting*, London: Secker and Warburg, 1993.

Whyte, Betsy, *The Yellow on the Broom: the early days of a traveller woman*, Edinburgh: Chambers, 1979.

Williamson, Duncan, *May the Devil walk behind ye!*, Edinburgh: Canongate, 1989.

— *The Horsieman* [autobiography], Edinburgh: Canongate, 1994.

Young, Andrew, *Poetical Works*, London: Secker and Warburg, 1975.

Anthologies

Brown, Hamish ed., *Poems of the Scottish Hills*, Aberdeen: Aberdeen University Press, 1982.

Dunn, Douglas ed., *The Faber Book of Twentieth-Century Scottish Poetry*, London: Faber and Faber, 1992.

Glen, Duncan, *Makars' Walk: walks in the Old Town of Edinburgh, with an anthology of poetry*, Edinburgh: Scottish Poetry Library and Edinburgh Old Town Trust, 1990.

Kerrigan, Catherine ed., *An Anthology of Scottish Women Poets*, Edinburgh: Edinburgh University Press, 1991.

Lyle, Emily ed., *Scottish Ballads*, Edinburgh: Canongate, 1994.

Stephen, Ian ed., *Siud an t-Eilean/There Goes the Island*, Stornoway: Acair, 1993.

Watson, Roderick ed., *The Poetry of Scotland, Gaelic, Scots and English, 1380–1980*, Edinburgh: Edinburgh University Press, 1995.

Whyte, Hamish ed., *Mungo's Tongues: Glasgow poems 1630–1990*, Edinburgh: Mainstream Publishing, 1993.

Further Reading

Burgess, Moira, *Imagine a city: Glasgow in fiction*, Glendaruel: Argyll Publishing, 1998.

Cameron, David Kerr, *The Ballad and the Plough*, London: Gollancz, 1978. North-East Scotland farm life and bothy ballads.

MacColl, Ewan and Seeger, Peggy, *Till Doomsday in the Afternoon*, Manchester: Manchester University Press, 1986. Lore, songs and way of life of Scotland's travelling people.

Mackenzie, Alexander, *The Prophecies of the Brahan Seer* [1899], Golspie: Sutherland Press, 1970.

McNeill, F. Marian, *The Silver Bough: a four-volume study of the national and local festivals of Scotland*, Glasgow: William MacLellan, 1957–68. Especially volume 1, 'Scottish folk-lore and folk-belief'.

Miles, Hugh and Jackman, Brian, *The Great Wood of Caledon*, Edinburgh: Colin Baxter, 1991. A splended book on the ecology of the Caledonian forest, with many photographs.

Murray, W. H., *Rob Roy MacGregor: his life and times* [1982], Edinburgh: Canongate, 1993.

Prebble, John, *The Highland Clearances*, London: Secker and Warburg, 1963.

Royle, Trevor, *Precipitous City: the story of literary Edinburgh*, Edinburgh: Mainstream Publishing, 1980.

Stott, Louis, *The Waterfalls of Scotland*, Aberdeen: Aberdeen University Press, 1987. A richly detailed book of maps, photographs, descriptions and legends.

Sources of Quotes

Grateful acknowledgement is made to the following sources for permission to reproduce material in this book previously published elsewhere. Every effort has been made to trace copyright holders, but if any have been inadvertently overlooked the publisher will be pleased to make the necessary arrangement at the first opportunity.

Foreword

page

ix   'Attempts to capture the spirit' from John Buchan, *The Literature of Tweeddale* (1925)

Introduction

page

1   'It requires great love of it deeply to read' from Hugh MacDiarmid: 'Scotland' in *Complete Poems* (Carcanet, 1993)

Chapter 1

page

5   'Cauld, cauld is Alnack' from Olive Fraser: 'Benighted to the foothills of the Cairngorms' in Hamish Brown ed. *Poems of the Scottish Hills* (Aberdeen University Press, 1982)

'Eastward the moor stretched flat and naked as a Sound' from Neil Munro: *The New Road* (B & W Publishing, 1994)

'that great stone' – complete poem – by G. F. Dutton: 'clach eanchainn' in *The Bare Abundance* (Bloodaxe Books)

6   'Bealach a' Chruidhe' from Rody Gorman: 'Leadan' in *Air a' Charbad fo Thalamh / On the Underground* (Polygon, 2000)

8   'The whole façade is clear' from Nan Shepherd: *The Living Mountain*, in *Grampian Quartet* (Canongate, 1996)

'Blows the wind today, and the sun and the rain are flying' from R. L. Stevenson: 'To S. R. Crockett' in *Collected Poems* (Rupert Hart-Davis, 1971)

9   'Wha gangs wi' us owre the hill' from William Soutar: 'Owre the Hill' in *Poems of William Soutar* by William Soutar (Scottish Academic Press, 1988)

'The stones were so near' from Neil Gunn: *Highland River* (Edinburgh: The Porpoise Press, 1937)

'Ye banks and braes of bonnie Doon' from Robert Burns: 'The Banks o' Doon' in *Poems and Songs* (Oxford University Press, 1969)

'Keen blaws the wind o'er the Braes o' Gleniffer' from Robert Tannahill: 'The Braes of Gleniffer' in W. M. Dixon ed. *The Edinburgh Book of Scottish Verse* (Meiklejohn and Holden, 1910)

10   'Foo aal's Bennachie? As aal's a man?' from Flora Garry: 'Foo aal's Bennachie?' in *Collected Poems* (Gordon Wright Publishing, 1995)

'The Outer Isles look as though' from Hugh MacDiarmid: 'Direadh III' in *Complete Poems* (Carcanet, 1993)

11   'Thar lochan fala clann nan daoine / Beyond the lochs of the blood of the children of men' from Sorley MacLean: 'An Cuilithionn / The Cuillin' in *Complete Poems* by Sorley MacLean (Carcanet, 1993)

'. . . this frieze of mountains filed' from Norman MacCaig: 'A Man in Assynt' in *Collected Poems* by Norman MacCaig published by Hogarth Press. Used by permission of The Random House Group

12   'An t-urram thar gach beinn / Honour past all bens' from Duncan Ban Macintyre: 'Moladh Beinn Dòbhrain / Praise of Ben Dorain', translated by Iain Crichton Smith, in Roderick Watson ed. *The Poetry of Scotland* (Edinburgh University Press, 1995)

13   'And I long to reach the crest' from Helen B. Cruickshank: 'Schiehallion' in *Collected Poems* (Reprographia, Edinburgh, 1971)

'This means, of course, Schiehallion in my mind' from Norman MacCaig: 'Landscape and I' in *Collected Poems* by Norman MacCaig published by Hogarth Press. Used by permission of The Random House Group

'So there I lie on the plateau' from Nan Shepherd: *The Living Mountain* in *Grampian Quartet* (Canongate, 1996)

Chapter 2

page

15   'Bhiodh òigridh ghreannmhor ri ceòl is dannsa / There'd be young folk singing and dancing' from Mairi Macpherson: 'Nuair bha mi og / When I was young', tr. Meg Bateman, in Catherine Kerrigan ed. *An Anthology of Scottish Women Poets* (Edinburgh University Press, 1991)

'. . . the dreadful Massacre of the McIvers' from A. L. Kennedy: 'The Role of Notable Silences in Scottish History' in *Night Geometry and the Garscadden Trains* (Polygon, 1990)

'plèan a' dol tarsainn / plane crossing' – complete poem – Aonghas MacNeacail: 'gleann fadamach / glen remote' in *an seachnadh / the avoiding* (Macdonald, 1986)

16   'In Kildonan there is today' from Neil Gunn: 'Caithness and Sutherland' in A. McCleery ed. *Landscape and Light* (Aberdeen University Press, 1987)

17   'Where have I heard a silence before' from Hugh MacDiarmid: 'The Glen of Silence' in *Complete Poems* by Hugh MacDiarmid (Carcanet, 1993)

'If you speak ill of the shepherds, speak it low' from Naomi Mitchison: 'Buchaille Etive Mor and Buchaille Etive Beag' in *The Cleansing of the Knife* (Canongate, 1978)

'To the right, not far on, is seen Ossian's Cave/Let me hope that William III' from Queen Victoria: *Highland Journals*, ed. David Duff (Lomond Books, 1994)

18   'The orders are that none be spared/Grey stone, if I were you' quoted from Seton Gordon: *Highways and Byways in the West Highlands* (Birlinn, 1995)

'forgotten of heaven and unfriendly to man' from Neil Munro: *John Splendid* (B & W Publishing, 1994)

19   'a charming stream, clear as crystal' from R. L. Stevenson: letter to J. M. Barrie, 1894. Quoted from Louis Stott: *Robert Louis Stevenson and the Highlands and Islands of Scotland* (Creag Darach Publications, Milton of Aberfoyle, 1992)

'Yet here the clatter' from 'In Any Glen'/'Stag, and fawn, and following hind' from 'Caenlochan', Helen B. Cruickshank in *Collected Poems* (Reprographia, Edinburgh, 1971)

20   '. . . meaning it may be so happit in snow/I have a greater drawing to the foolish youth' from J. M. Barrie: *Farewell Miss Julie Logan* (Scottish Academic Press, 1989)

'That evening as I took the path over the Point' from Neil Gunn: *Off in a boat* (House of Lochar, 1998)

21   'O Glen Etive, O Glen Etive' from Kenneth MacLeod: 'Deirdre's Farewell to Alba' in Marjory Kennedy-Fraser ed. *Songs of the Hebrides,* vol. 4

'I am with Alba – with Deirdre – now' from Hugh MacDiarmid: 'Direadh III' in *Complete Poems* by Hugh MacDiarmid (Carcanet, 1993)

Chapter 3

page

23   'Something vast and dark' from John Buchan: *Witch Wood* (Houghton Mifflin, 1927)

'Are these bears? Mist. Wolves? Peat. Is there a sun?' from Edwin Morgan: 'Silva Caledonia' in *Collected Poems* by Edwin Morgan (Carcanet, 1990)

'Tagh seilach nan allt/Choose the willow of the streams': traditional, in Alexander Carmichael ed. *Carmina Gadelica*, vol. 4 (Oliver and Boyd, 1940)

24   'The variety of sun and shade is here unknown/The country is totally denuded of its wood' from Samuel Johnson: *A Journey to the Western Islands of Scotland* (Yale University Press, 1977)

25   'Here and there upon some stream a picturesque saw mill was situated' from Elizabeth Grant of Rothiemurchus: *Memoirs of a Highland Lady*, vol. 1 (Canongate, 1988)

'The first pine to the second said' from R. L. Stevenson: 'The Disputatious Pines' quoted from Louis Stott: *Robert Louis Stevenson and the Highlands and Islands of Scotland* (Creag Darach Publications, Milton of Aberfoyle, 1992)

26   'Rowan tree and red threid' – traditional verse

''s tha mo ghaol aig Allt Hallaig/and my love is at the Burn of Hallaig' from Sorley MacLean: 'Hallaig' in *Complete Poems* by Sorley MacLean (Carcanet, 1993)

27   'It fell about the Martinmas' from 'The Wife of Usher's Well' in William Beattie ed. *Border Ballads* (Penguin, 1952)

'While the mistletoe bats on Errol's aik' – traditional verse

28   'The two rivers, Etterick and Yarrow' from James Hogg: *Highland Tours* (Byway Books, Hawick, 1981)

'decorous landscape/Something cold seemed to have descended' from John Buchan: *Witch Wood* (Houghton Mifflin, 1927)

Chapter 4

page

31   'This darksome burn, horseback brown' from Gerard Manley Hopkins: 'Inversnaid' in *Poems of Gerard Manley Hopkins* (Oxford University Press, 1975)

'I've led you on by my garrulous banks, babbling' from Liz Lochhead: 'What the Pool Said, on Midsummer's Day' in *Dreaming Frankenstein* (Polygon, 1984)

'O you'll tak the high road and I'll tak the low road' – traditional song

33   'Says Tweed to Till' – traditional verse

'Here and there in the moss' from Nan Shepherd: *The Living Mountain* in *Grampian Quartet* (Canongate, 1996)

34   'All at once before him again was the tiny stream' from Neil Gunn: *Highland River* (Edinburgh: The Porpoise Press, 1937)

'I mind o' the Ponnage Pule' – complete poem – Helen B. Cruickshank: 'The Ponnage Pule' in *Collected Poems* (Reprographia, Edinburgh, 1971)

35   'Pride of play in a flourish of eddies' from Hugh MacDiarmid: 'The Point of Honour' in *Complete Poems* by Hugh MacDiarmid (Carcanet, 1993)

'Nan d' rachadh agam/If I could be anything I wanted' from Rody Gorman: 'Uisge Spe/Spey Water' in *Air a' Charbad fo Thalamh/On the Underground* (Polygon, 2000)

36   'Whaur sall I enter the Promised Land' from John Buchan: 'The South Countrie' in *Poems Scots and English* (Thomas Nelson, 1953)

'Annan, Tweed and Clyde' – traditional verse

'Mind ye, a man could cross Clyde, if he wasna feart' from Robert MacLellan: 'Sunnyside' in *Linmill Stories* (Canongate, 1990)

37   'And through thy heart, as through a dream' from Alexander Smith: 'Glasgow', published 1857, quoted from Hamish Whyte ed. *Mungo's Tongues* (Mainstream, 1993)

'Where down at once the foaming waters pour' from John Wilson : 'Clyde', published 1803, quoted from Duncan Glen: *Splendid Lanarkshire* (Akros, 1997)

'The majesty and strength of the water' from Dorothy Wordsworth: *Recollections of a Tour Made in Scotland* (Edinburgh: David Douglas, 1894)

38   'Here, foaming down the skelvy rocks' from Robert Burns: 'The Humble Petition of Bruar Water to the Noble Duke of Athole' in *Poems and Songs* (Oxford University Press, 1969)

'The wind was basins slopping over' from Norman MacCaig: 'Falls of Measach' in *Collected Poems* by Norman MacCaig published by Hogarth Press. Used by permission of The Random House Group

'Where deep deep down and far within' from Walter Scott: 'Marmion' in *Collected Poems* (Oxford Standard Authors)

39   'The lane hills and the mune' from Sydney Goodsir Smith: 'Omens' in *Collected Poems* (John Calder, 1975) © John Calder (Publishers) Ltd 1975, reproduced by permission of The Calder Educational Trust.

Chapter 5

page

41 'Islands are bits of the land' – complete poem – Angus Martin: 'Islands' in *The Larch Plantation* (Macdonald, 1990)
'From the lone shieling of the misty island' published anonymously 1829
'Strange to see it – how as we lean over' from Iain Crichton Smith: 'The Departing Island' in *Selected Poems* (Carcanet, 1985)

42 'Look whaur the mist reiks aff the split craigs' from Robert McLellan: 'Arran Burn' in *Sweet Largie Bay and Arran Burn* (Akros, 1977)
'Bharrain, Bhreac, Tarsuinn' from Robin Fulton: 'Arran Haiku', quoted in Hamish Whyte ed. *An Arran Anthology* (Mercat Press, 1997)
© Robin Fulton, reproduced by kind permission of Mr Fulton
'There was a kind of mark in the clouds' from Naomi Mitchison: 'In the 'Plane' in *Five Men and a Swan* (Allen and Unwin, 1957)

43 'O Eilein mhoir, Eilein mo ghaoil/O great island, island of my love' from Sorley MacLean: 'An t-Eilean/The Island' in
Collected Poems by Sorley MacLean (Carcanet, 1993)

44 'A woman of middle stature' from Samuel Johnson: *A Journey to the Western Islands of Scotland* (London: W. Strahan, 1775)
'The room where we lay was a celebrated one' from James Boswell: *The Journal of a Tour to the Hebrides* (Heinemann, 1936)
'Speed, bonnie boat' from Sir Harold Boulton: 'Skye Boat Song', first published 1885
'Sing me a song of a lad that is gone' from R. L. Stevenson: 'Skye Boat Song' in *Collected Poems* (Rupert Hart–Davis, 1971)

45 'There was a great drinking-hall at Orphir' from *Orkneyinga Saga*, tr. Hermann Palsson and Paul Edwards (Penguin, 1981)
'Over the sound a ship so slow would pass' from Edwin Muir: 'Childhood' in *Collected Poems* by Edwin Muir
(Faber and Faber Ltd., 1960) reproduced by permission of Faber and Faber. US: Oxford University Press
'Light is the dominating factor in its scenery' from Eric Linklater: 'Orkney' in George Scott-Moncrieff ed. *Scottish Country*
(Wishart Books, 1935)

46 'The winter lift is glintan doun' – complete poem – Robert Rendall: 'Celestial Kinsmen' in Neil Dickson ed. *An Island Shore*
(Orkney Press, Kirkwall, 1990)
'My father passed with his penny letters' from George Mackay Brown: 'Hamnavoe' in *Selected Poems 1954–83* (John Murray, 1991)
reproduced by permission of John Murray (Publishers) Ltd.
'Those huge apostle feet' from George Mackay Brown: 'The Twelve Piers of Hamnavoe' in *Poems New and Selected* (Hogarth Press, 1971)

47 'Oot bewast da Horn o Papa' from 'Da Sang o da Papa Men'/'a glöd o blue and gold' from 'Hjalta'/'You see noo, every saison' from
'Kvarna Farna', T. A. Robertson in *Collected Poems of Vagaland* (Shetland Times, Lerwick, 1975) reproduced by kind permission of
Mrs Martha Robertson

48 'In the voar number of the *New Shetlander*' from Robert Alan Jamieson: *Thin Wealth* (Polygon, 1986)
'But it was the fine bareness of Lewis' from Iain Crichton Smith: 'Eight Songs for a New Ceilidh (2)' in *Selected Poems* (Carcanet, 1985)

49 'Is gann gu faca mi Hòl am bliadhna/I hardly noticed Hol this year' – complete poem – Derick Thomson:
'Hol, Air Atharrachd/Hol, Changed' in *Smeur an Dochais/Bramble of Hope* (Canongate, 1991) reproduced by permission
of Canongate Press

50 'It is a remote democracy, where men' from Douglas Dunn: 'St Kilda's Parliament' in *Selected Poems 1964–83* (Faber and Faber, 1986)
reproduced by permission from Faber and Faber Ltd
'I could have sworn I saw a shape' from Nan Shepherd: *The Living Mountain* in *Grampian Quartet* (Canongate, 1996)
'"Do you think," asked Art' from Neil Gunn: *The Green Isle of the Great Deep* (Souvenir Press, 1975)

Chapter 6

page

53 'Na tuinn chaoirgheal mu Gharbhail/Waves blazing with foam round Garvel' from George Campbell Hay: 'Luinneag/It was
the hardness of the wind' in *Collected Poems and Songs*, ed. Michel Byrne (Edinburgh University Press, 2000)
'Here lay a fair fat land' from Andrew Young: 'Culbin Sands' in *Selected Poems* (Carcanet Press Ltd.)
'Na ceòsanaich àrda, chroma/The wide-skirted curving waters' from Alasdair MacMhaighstir Alasdair:
'Birlinn Chlann Raghnaill/Clanranald's Galley', tr. Iain Crichton Smith, in Roderick Watson ed. *The Poetry of Scotland*
(Edinburgh University Press, 1995)

54 'Branches rocking, waves of shadow, all the trees' from George Campbell Hay: 'The Kerry Shore' in *Collected Poems and Songs*,
ed. Michel Byrne (Edinburgh University Press, 2000)

55 'An sic a sight A'm never seen!' from T. A. Robertson: 'Da Western Waves' in *Collected Poems of Vagaland* (Shetland Times,
Lerwick, 1975) reproduced by kind permission of Mrs Martha Robertson
'He had heard of a Gaelic poem' from Neil Gunn: *The Silver Darlings* (Faber and Faber, 1969)
'O ragin' wind' – complete poem – Helen B. Cruickshank: 'Overdue' in *Collected Poems* (Reprographia, Edinburgh, 1971)

56 'I cast my line in Largo Bay' from 'The Boatie Rows' – traditional
'The herrin' iss a great, great mystery' from Neil Munro: 'Herring – a Gossip' in *Para Handy*, ed. B. D. Osborne and R. Armstrong
(Birlinn, 1992)
'You were gutting herring in distant Yarmouth' from Iain Crichton Smith: 'To My Mother' in *Selected Poems* (Carcanet, 1985)
'An gaire mar chraiteachan salainn/Their laughter like a sprinkling of salt' from Derick Thomson:
'Clann-Nighean an Sgadain/The Herring Girls' in *Creachadh na clarsaich/Plundering the harp* (Macdonald, 1982)

57 'The anchor chains were red hot' from John MacDougall Hay: *Gillespie* (Canongate, 1983)
'Calum thonder, long's the night to your thinking' from George Campbell Hay: 'To a Loch Fyne Fisherman' in *Collected Poems and Songs*,
ed. Michel Byrne (Edinburgh University Press, 2000)

58 'She's stieve, thrawn, light, quick' from George Campbell Hay: 'Seeker, Reaper' in *Collected Poems and Songs,* ed. Michel Byrne
(Edinburgh University Press, 2000)
'And at last they saw the green colour' from Naomi Mitchison and Denis Macintosh: *Men and Herring* (Serif Books, Edinburgh, 1949)
'Green Waters' from Ian Hamilton Finlay: 'Green Waters' in Alec Finlay ed. *Green Waters: An Anthology of Boats and Voyages*
(Polygon Pocketbooks 1, 1999)

59 'Mr Stevenson happened to observe' from Walter Scott: *The Voyage of the Pharos* (Scottish Library Association, 1998)
'They hear no sound, the swell is strong' from Robert Southey: 'The Inchcape Rock' in I. and P. Opie ed. *Oxford Book of Narrative Verse*
(Oxford University Press, 1983)

60 'Whenever I smell salt water/For love of lovely words, and for the sake' by R. L. Stevenson
'The tide caught the brig/dry-shod, or at the least by wading' from R. L. Stevenson: *Kidnapped* (Penguin, 1994)

61 'The night, though we were so little past midsummer from R. L. Stevenson: 'The Merry Men', originally published 1884–7
    in Douglas Gifford ed. *Scottish Short Stories 1800–1900* (Calder and Boyars, 1971)
    'Like curs a glance has brought to heel' from Wilfrid Gibson: 'Flannan Isle' in Walter de la Mare ed. *Come Hither* (Constable, 1928)
    reproduced by permission of Constable & Robinson Publishing Ltd

Chapter 7
page
65 'The kirk, in a gale of psalms, went heaving through' from George Mackay Brown: 'Hamnavoe' in *Selected Poems 1954–83*
    (John Murray, 1991) reproduced by permission of John Murray (Publishers) Ltd
    'Nearby the bit loch was a circle of stones' from Lewis Grassic Gibbon: *Sunset Song* (Canongate, 1988)
    'The wine of the burn of the Annat' from Duncan Ban MacIntyre: 'In Praise of Ben Dorain'
66 '"The old folk call it Chapelhill"' from Neil Gunn: *The Silver Darlings* (Faber and Faber, 1969)
    'If thou would'st view fair Melrose aright' from Walter Scott: 'The Lay of the Last Minstrel' in *Collected Poems* (Oxford Standard Authors)
67 'The auld kirk stood as crouse as a cat/a brave kirk' from Walter Scott: *Rob Roy* (originally published 1818)
    'The seats are so closely packed' from Robert Southey: *Journal of a Tour in Scotland in 1819*, quoted from
    Simon Berry and Hamish Whyte ed. *Glasgow Observed* (John Donald, 1987)
    'I could hardly walk through the building' from Harriet Beecher Stowe: *Sunny Memories of Foreign Lands* (1854), quoted from
    Simon Berry and Hamish Whyte ed. *Glasgow Observed* (John Donald, 1987)
    'The clouds were rolling in black and lowering masses' from John Galt: *The Entail* (Oxford World's Classics, 1913)
    'a sturdy Gothic ark/the whole landscape tilted like a board' from Alasdair Gray: *Lanark* (Canongate, 1981)
68 'The Magnustide long swords of rain' from George Mackay Brown: 'Elegy' in *Selected Poems 1954–83* (John Murray, 1991)
    reproduced by permission of John Murray (Publishers) Ltd.
    'Hidden away among these yews were kirk and manse' from Lewis Grassic Gibbon: *Sunset Song* (Canongate, 1988)
    'Clouds of smoke on the hill' from Helen B. Cruickshank: 'Spring in the Mearns' in *Collected Poems* (Reprographia, Edinburgh, 1971)
69 'Here's the church and here's the steeple' – traditional rhyme
    'Hear how he clears the points o' Faith' from Robert Burns: 'The Holy Fair' in *Poems and Songs* (Oxford University Press, 1969)
    'Morn, with bonnie purpie-smiles' from 'Auld Reekie'/Wanwordy, crazy, dinsome thing from 'To the Tron-Kirk Bell',
    Robert Fergusson in *Selected Poems* (Birlinn, 2000)
70 'Pillar to pillar, stane to stane' from Lewis Spence: 'The Prows o' Reekie' in Douglas Young ed. *Scottish Verse 1851–1951* (Nelson, 1952)
    'squealed like ony gaits' from 'Christ's Kirk on the Green' (15–16th century, author unknown) in Roderick Watson ed.
    The Poetry of Scotland (Edinburgh University Press, 1995)
    'How monie hearts this day converts' from Robert Burns: 'The Holy Fair' in *Poems and Songs* (Oxford University Press, 1969)
71 'They made His day a rookery o kirks' from Tom Scott: 'Fergus' (10th Stanza) from *The Shorter Collected Poems* by Tom Scott
    published by Chapman Publishing, 4 Broughton Place, Edinburgh EH1 3RX, reproduced with permission
    'Oh to be at Crowdieknowe' – complete poem – Hugh MacDiarmid: 'Crowdieknowe' in *Complete Poems* by Hugh MacDiarmid
    (Carcanet, 1993)
    'But Lord, remember me and mine' from Robert Burns: 'Holy Willie's Prayer' in *Poems and Songs* (Oxford University Press, 1969)
72 'When a'body's thochts is set on their ain salvation' from Violet Jacob: 'Tam i' the Kirk' in *The Scottish Poems of Violet Jacob*
    (Oliver and Boyd, 1944)
    'Seem'd all on fire that chapel proud' from Walter Scott: 'The Lay of the Last Minstrel' in *Collected Poems* (Oxford Standard Authors)
    'The interior was as ornate as any cathedral's/Sounds like some builders I know/This is where the spaceship is' from Ian Rankin:
    Set in Darkness (Orion, 2000)

Chapter 8
page
75 'This is my country' from Alexander Gray: 'Scotland' in *Selected Poems* (William Maclellan, 1948)
    'O prejudice!' from John Keats written 1818, quoted in Edward Thomas: *A Literary Pilgrim* (Webb and Bower, Exeter, 1985)
    'howckan in a sheugh' from Robert Burns: 'The Twa Dogs' in *Poems and Songs* (Oxford University Press, 1969)
    'Across the heavy-laden grainfields' from Hugh MacDiarmid: 'Direadh II' in *Complete Poems* by Hugh MacDiarmid (Carcanet, 1993)
    'She promised weel aneuch – a heavy crap' from Flora Garry: 'Ae Mair Hairst' in *Collected Poems* (Gordon Wright Publishing,
    Edinburgh, 1995)
76 'A maiden sang sweetly' from 'Crodh Chailean' – this translation by Alexander Stewart in W. M. Dixon ed.
    The Edinburgh Book of Scottish Verse (Meiklejohn and Holden, 1910)
    'I had been born there, my minnie said' from Robert McLellan: 'The Pownie' in *Linmill Stories* (Canongate, 1990)
    'He cut a sappy sucker from the muckle rodden-tree' from Charles Murray: 'The Whistle' in *Hamewith: Complete Poems*
    (Aberdeen University Press, 1979)
77 'Hoot, Mains, hae mind, I'm doon for you some sma' thing wi' the bank' from Charles Murray: 'Dockens Afore his Peers' in
    Hamewith: Complete Poems (Aberdeen University Press, 1979)
    'I gaed in by Turra market' – traditional bothy ballad, various sources
78 'There's a fairm up in Cairnie' – traditional bothy ballad, various sources
    'You could look at the beauty of your quine' from David Toulmin: 'Aikey Brae' in *Collected Short Stories*
    (Gordon Wright, Edinburgh, 1992)
    'a hosepipe and stirrup-pump/Below me and half a mile to my right' from Duncan McLean: *Blackden* (Secker and Warburg, 1994)
79 'This farm has undone my enjoyment of myself' Robert Burns, letter to his brother Gilbert 1790, quoted in James A. Mackay:
    Burns-Lore of Dumfries and Galloway (Alloway Publishing, Ayr, 1988)
    'Consulting several tours through Scotland' James Hogg (originally published 1802) in *Highland Tours* (Byway Books, Hawick, 1981)
    'Weel, syne we hae the kitchie deem, that milks an' mak's the maet' from Charles Murray: 'Dockens Afore his Peers' in
    Hamewith: Complete Poems (Aberdeen University Press, 1979)
    'I look far ower by Ythanside' from Flora Garry: 'Bennygoak' in *Collected Poems* (Gordon Wright Publishing, Edinburgh, 1995)
80 'Two Chrisses there were/And then a queer thought came to her' from Lewis Grassic Gibbon: *Sunset Song* (Canongate, 1988)
    '. . . one morning on his road to school' from Jessie Kesson: *Glitter of Mica* (Paul Harris, Edinburgh, 1982)
81 'Look at that heuch' from Lewis Grassic Gibbon: 'Clay' in *A Scots Hairst*, ed. Ian S. Munro (Hutchinson, 1967)

Chapter 9

page

83   'Living in the Big House is being' from Naomi Mitchison: 'Living in a Village' in *The Cleansing of the Knife* (Canongate, 1978)

'Oh the auld hoose, the auld hoose' from Carolina Oliphant: 'The Auld Hoose'

84   'The old house had a few low rooms' from Elizabeth Grant of Rothiemurchus: *Memoirs of a Highland Lady*, vol. 1 (Canongate, 1988)

'He pass'd where Newark's stately tower' from Walter Scott: 'The Lay of the Last Minstrel' in *Collected Poems* (Oxford Standard Authors)

85   'Quhitever shite drappt oot dy privvies' from Robert Alan Jamieson: 'T' Scallwa Castle' in *Shoormal* (Polygon, 1986)

'Whaur Mary and I meet amang the green bushes' from Walter Watson: 'The Braes o' Bedlay' quoted in Hugh Macdonald: *Historical, Biographical and Literary Sketches of Glasgow and Lanarkshire* (1904)

86   'This wot all ye whom it concerns' from Robert Burns: 'Extempore Verses on Dining with Lord Daer' in *Poems and Songs* (Oxford University Press, 1969)

'Ye see yon birkie ca'd a lord' from Robert Burns: 'For a' that and a' that' in *Poems and Songs* (Oxford University Press, 1969)

'Whoe'er he be that sojourns here' from Robert Burns: 'Epigram' in *Poems and Songs* (Oxford University Press, 1969)

'He knew, and she knew, and each knew that the other knew' from Naomi Mitchison: *The Big House* (Canongate, 1987)

87   '. . . saying why on earth was I playing at farming' from Naomi Mitchison: *Among You Taking Notes* (Gollancz, 1985)

'Dir usliss deevils here an dere' from J. J. Haldane Burgess: 'Dokkins' in Douglas Young ed. *Scottish Verse 1851–1951* (Nelson, 1952)

'There's a puckle lairds in the auld house' from William Soutar: 'The Auld House' in *Poems of William Soutar* by William Soutar (Scottish Academic Press, 1988)

Chapter 10

page

91   'At night we came to Banff' from Samuel Johnson: *A Journey to the Western Islands of Scotland* (Penguin, 1984)

'You did not live to see' from George Mackay Brown: 'In Memoriam' in *Selected Poems 1954–83* (John Murray, 1991) reproduced by permission of John Murray (Publishers) Ltd

'. . . most of the other small towns' from Edwin Muir: *Scottish Journey* (Heinemann and Gollancz, 1935)

92   'Here I am once more at the bottom of this pit of dullness' letter from Jane Welsh to Eliza Stodart, 1824, quoted in Alan Bold: *Scotland: a literary guide* (Routledge, 1989)

'Nae matter hoo faur I've travelled sinsyn'e from Hugh MacDiarmid: 'Dedication to *Stony Limits and Other Poems*' in *Complete Poems* by Hugh MacDiarmid (Carcanet, 1993)

'The town's bell rang through the dark' from Neil Munro: *The Daft Days* (Blackwood, 1924)

'It was agreed among the heritors' from John Galt: *Annals of the Parish* (Mercat Press, 1994)

93   'Thrums is the name I give here to a handful of houses' from J. M. Barrie: *Auld Licht Idylls* (1888)

'There's an auld wife bides in Kirrie – set her up! a pridefu' cratur' from Violet Jacob: 'Kirrie' in *The Scottish Poems of Violet Jacob* (Oliver and Boyd, 1944)

94   'They were standing at the Cross to enjoy their Saturday at e'en' from George Douglas Brown: *The House with the Green Shutters* (Penguin, 1985)

95   'And who in all Drumorty would think' from Lorna Moon: 'The Corp' in *Doorways in Drumorty* (Gourdas House, Aberdeen, 1981)

'Life is dull. There is little alternative employment' from Naomi Mitchison: 'Rural Reconstruction' article in *The New Scotland* (1942)

'You could sum up the Highland way of life' from Naomi Mitchison: *Lobsters on the Agenda* (House of Lochar, 1998)

96   '. . . a town hunched round a harbour like a classical amphitheatre from Alan Warner: *The Sopranos* (Jonathan Cape, 1998)

Chapter 11

page

99   'An' the flame-tappit furnaces staun' in a raw' from Janet Hamilton: 'Gartsherrie' (first published c. 1850)

'I had gone as far as the Herd's house' James Watt related this in 1813, quoted in H. W. Dickinson: *James Watt* (1935)

'Of *Crawford-Moor*, born in *Leadhill*' from Allan Ramsay 'To the Whin-Bush Club' quoted in Alan Bold: *Scotland: a literary guide* (Routledge, 1989)

'It had been often remarked by ingenious men' from John Galt: *Annals of the Parish* (Mercat Press, 1994)

100 'Wi' something that the learn'd ca' *steam*' from William Muir: 'The Steam Barge'

'This grey town' from John Davidson: 'A Ballad in Blank Verse on the Making of a Poet' in Douglas Young ed. *Scottish Verse 1851–1951* (Nelson, 1952)

'Mighty furnaces are flaring' from James Macfarlan: 'The Wanderer', originally published 1857, quoted from Hamish Whyte ed. *Mungo's Tongues* (Mainstream, 1993)

'unsightly brick-lanes smoke' from Thomas Campbell: 'Lines on Revisiting a Scottish River'. Originally published 1827. Quoted from Hamish Whyte ed. *Mungo's Tongues* (Mainstream, 1993)

'Oot-owre the auld brig, up to sweet Simmerlee' from Janet Hamilton: 'Simmerlee' in her *Poems and Ballads* (1868)

101 'I got a job on the railway' from Patrick MacGill: *Children of the Dead End* (Caliban, Horsham, 1982)

'they fairly mak' ye work' from Mary Brooksbank: 'Oh Dear Me' in *Sidlaw Breezes* (Dundee: David Winter, 1982)

'What care some gentry if they're weel' from Ellen Johnston: 'The Last Sark' in *An Anthology of Scottish Women Poets* ed. Catherine Kerrigan (Edinburgh University Press, 1991)

'Crawlin' about like a snail in the mud' from Joe Corrie: 'The Image o' God' in *The Image o' God and other poems* (1937)

'Yeah, tighten that bolt, bud!' from Jeff Torrington: *The Devil's Carousel* (Secker and Warburg, 1996). Used by permission of The Random House Group Limited

102 'For an hour you sit at the machine / The kiln is where cley either hardens' from William McIlvanney: *The Kiln* (Hodder and Stoughton, 1996)

'Up on deck the air was cool, cool grey' from Alexander Trocchi: *Young Adam* (John Calder, 1983)

'knitting and riveting' from Colin Donati: 'The Forth Bridge 1887'

103 'Yard after yard passed by' from George Blake: *The Shipbuilders* (Faber and Faber, 1935)

'The great sick Clyde shivers in its bed' from 'Glasgow Sonnet vi' / 'The marshy scurf crept up to our machine' from 'The Coin', Edwin Morgan in *Collected Poems* by Edwin Morgan (Carcanet, 1993)

Chapter 12

page

105 'I saw rain falling and the rainbow drawn' from R. L. Stevenson: 'To My Wife', dedication to *Weir of Hermiston* (Dent Everyman, 1925)

'a disappointed spinster . . .' [and remaining quotes in this para] from Lewis Grassic Gibbon: 'Glasgow' in *A Scots Hairst*, ed. Ian S. Munro (Hutchinson, 1967)

'the palace of Scottish blackguardism' from Lord Cockburn: *Circuit Journeys*. Originally published 1844. Quoted from A. Cran and J. Robertson ed. *Dictionary of Scottish Quotations* (Mainstream, 1996)

'Where have I seen a human being looking' from Hugh MacDiarmid: 'Glasgow' in *Complete Poems* by Hugh MacDiarmid (Carcanet, 1993)

'. . . if I was tired or ill' from Edwin Muir: *An Autobiography* (Canongate Classics, 1954)

106 'Behold there is nurro jakes in the whole kingdom' from Tobias Smollett: *The Expedition of Humphry Clinker* (Edward Arnold, 1973)

'Blyth Aberdeen, thou beryl of all towns' from William Dunbar: 'To Aberdein'. Quoted from A. Cran and J. Robertson ed. *Dictionary of Scottish Quotations* (Mainstream, 1996)

'. . . And hirplan hame half-drouned wi the weicht o herrin' from Alexander Scott: 'Heart of Stone' in *Collected Poems* (Mercat Press, 1994)

'Aberdeen, I constantly evoke' – complete poem – Iain Crichton Smith: 'Aberdeen University 1945–1949: 6' in *Collected Poems* by Iain Crichton Smith (Carcanet, 1985)

107 'Glitter of mica at the windy corners' from G. S. Fraser: 'Hometown Elegy' in *Poems* (Leicester University Press, 1981)

'O the regret as a body growes auld!' from Jessie Kesson: 'A Scarlet Goon' in *Somewhere Beyond*, ed. Isobel Murray (B & W Publishing, 2000), reproduced by permission of John Johnson Ltd

108 'Since the early seventies, the area's population' from Ian Rankin: *Black and Blue* (Orion, 1997)

'Chaos was a rare visitor to this orderly city' from Leila Aboulela: *The Translator* (Polygon, 1999)

'Perth will be brought low' from James Young Geddes: 'The Glory has Departed' in W. N. Herbert and Richard Price ed. *Duende* (Gairfish, Dundee, 1991)

109 'A flame, as Lord Byron has said' from 'Brief Autobiography'/'As soon as the catastrophe came to be known' from 'The Tay Bridge Disaster', William McGonagall: *Poetic Gems* (David Winter, Dundee, 1950)

'Well Eh luked up at grey gulls skriekan' from W. N. Herbert: 'Seagull Blues' in *Cabaret McGonagall* (Bloodaxe Books, 1996)

'Such dusky grandeur cloth'd the height' from Walter Scott: 'Marmion' in *Collected Poems* (Oxford Standard Authors)

110 'No sculptured Marble here, nor pompous lay' from Robert Burns: 'Epitaph: Here lies Robert Fergusson, poet' in *Poems and Songs* (Oxford University Press, 1969)

'Auld Reekie! wale o' ilka town' from Robert Fergusson: 'Auld Reekie' in *Selected Poems* (Birlinn, 2000)

'O thou, my elder brother in misfortune' from Robert Burns: 'On Fergusson' in *Poems and Songs* (Oxford University Press, 1969)

'I had always a great sense of kinship with poor Robert Fergusson' by R. L. Stevenson

111 'Canongait kirkyaird in the failing year' – complete poem – Robert Garioch: 'At Robert Fergusson's Grave' in *Complete Poetical Works* (Macdonald, 1983)

'one of the vilest climates under heaven' from R. L. Stevenson: *Edinburgh: Picturesque Notes* (Barnes and Noble, 1993)

'Man is not truly one, but truly two' from R. L. Stevenson: *The Strange Case of Dr Jekyll and Mr Hyde* (Penguin, 1979)

'It was then that Miss Brodie looked beautiful and fragile' from Muriel Spark: *The Prime of Miss Jean Brodie* (Penguin, 1965)

112 'In simmer, whan aa sorts foregether' from Robert Garioch: 'Embro to the Ploy' in *Complete Poetical Works* (Macdonald, 1983)

'At the bus stop, ah realised what a sweltering hot day it had become' from Irvine Welsh: *Trainspotting* (Secker and Warburg, 1993)

113 'Draw thy fierce streams of blinding ore' from Alexander Smith: 'Glasgow', originally published 1857, quoted from Hamish Whyte ed. *Mungo's Tongues* (Mainstream, 1993)

'Eh, ma citie o raucle sang' from John Kincaid: 'A Glesca Rhapsodie' in *Fowrsom Reel* (Caledonian Press, Glasgow, 1949)

'A Victorian row "commanding a beautiful view . . ."' from Guy McCrone: *Wax Fruit* (Constable, 1947)

'with its beautiful flowers and trees so green' from William McGonagall: 'Glasgow' in *Poetic Gems* (David Winter, Dundee, 1950)

'Deep in its rut the river shed' from Ian Hamilton: 'News of the World' in Hamish Whyte ed. *Mungo's Tongues* (Mainstream, 1993)

114 'Battles and sex are the only free diversions in slum life' from Alexander McArthur and H. Kingsley Long: *No Mean City* (Corgi, 1957)

'. . . green May, and the slow great blocks rising' from Edwin Morgan: 'The Second Life' in *Collected Poems* by Edwin Morgan (Carcanet, 1993)

'Having so cursorily dismantled the community's heart' from Jeff Torrington: *Swing Hammer Swing!* (Secker and Warburg, 1992)

115 '. . . God Glasgow it's glorious' from Donny O'Rourke: 'Great Western Road' in Hamish Whyte ed. *Mungo's Tongues* (Mainstream, 1993)

'It groans and shakes, contracts and grows again' – complete poem – Edwin Morgan: 'Glasgow Sonnet ix' in *Collected Poems* by Edwin Morgan (Carcanet, 1993)

Chapter 13

page

119 'After *Cill Osbran* closed up to Closeburn' from William Neill: 'Map Makers' in *Wild Places* (Luath Press, 1985)

'In this still place, remote from men' from William Wordsworth: 'Glen Almain, or the Narrow Glen' in Dorothy Wordsworth: *Recollections of a Tour Made in Scotland* (Edinburgh: David Douglas, 1894)

120 'found names, and stories, and phrases' Samuel Johnson quoted by James Boswell in *The Journal of a Tour to the Hebrides* (Heinemann, 1936)

'composers and writers and patrons of Gaelic' from John Carswell 'Epistle to the Earl of Argyll' in *Book of Common Order* [1567]

121 'Brighde nan gealachos/Brigit of the white feet' from Alexander Carmichael ed. *Carmina Gadelica*, vol. 3 (Oliver and Boyd, 1940)

'Saint Bride, Saint Bride, send me my kye again!' from David Lyndsay: *Ane Satyre of the Thrie Estaitis* (Canongate Classics)

'There's the tree that never grew' – traditional rhyme

122 '. . . The cell /is filled with song' from Edwin Morgan: 'Colloquy in Glaschu' in *Collected Poems* by Edwin Morgan (Carcanet, 1993)

'Far am bi bo bidh bean /Where there will be a cow' – traditional saying

'I mo chridhe, I mo ghraidh /In Iona of my heart, Iona of my love' – traditional verse

123 'Ancient exalted seed-scatterer whom time gave no progenitor' from Edwin Morgan: *The Maker on High* (Mariscat Press, Glasgow, 1997)

'Buried on St Michael's night' from Walter Scott: 'The Lay of the Last Minstrel' in *Collected Poems* (Oxford Standard Authors)

'Tide what may betide' – traditional saying

124 'It was mirk mirk night, there was nae stern light' from 'Thomas the Rhymer' in William Beattie ed. *Border Ballads* (Penguin, 1952)

'a road on every hill' [and other prophecies quoted in this and next para] from Alexander Mackenzie: *The Prophecies of the Brahan Seer* (Sutherland Press, Golspie, 1970)

Chapter 14
page

127 'That ribbon of smoke' from Sean Rafferty: 'Salathiel's Song' in *Collected Poems* (Carcanet, 1995)

'O come all youse hawkers, you men of the road' from Duncan Williamson: 'The Hawker's Lament' in *The Horsieman* (Canongate, 1994) reproduced by permission of Canongate Press.

'Princes, they ruled in our street' from George Mackay Brown: 'Tinkers' in *Poems New and Selected* (Hogarth Press, 1971)

128 '. . . a gang of tinklers, that made horn spoons and mended bellows' from John Galt: *Annals of the Parish* (Mercat Press, 1994)

'The gipsies they came to Lord Cassilis' yett' from 'Johnnie Faa' in William Beattie ed. *Border Ballads* (Penguin, 1952)

129 'One word could have many meanings' from Betsy Whyte: *The Yellow on the Broom* (Chambers, 1979)

130 '. . . the oral literature and song of the Travelling People' – Hamish Henderson in Timothy Neat: *The Summer Walkers* (Canongate, 1996)

'We were allowed to look at them, admire them' from Duncan Williamson: *The Horsieman* (Canongate, 1994)

'There's jist the tent to leave, lad' from Violet Jacob: 'The Last o' the Tinkler' in *The Scottish Poems of Violet Jacob* (Oliver and Boyd, 1944)

'Rognvald who stalks round Corse with his stick' from George Mackay Brown: 'Ikey on the People of Hellya' in *Poems New and Selected* (Hogarth Press, 1971)

131 '. . . Mostly all the tinker children came to my school in winter' from Naomi Mitchison: 'A Matter of Behaviour' in *A Girl Must Live* (Richard Drew, 1990)

'The demand for tin dishes fell away' from Duncan Williamson: *The Horsieman* (Canongate, 1994)

Chapter 15
page

133 'I do not much like extermination' from Hugh Miller: *The Cruise of the Betsey* (1858)

'Those people who were cleared by you off the Larg sheep farm' from Neil Gunn: *Butcher's Broom* (Souvenir Press, 1977)

'The interior of [Sutherland] was thus improved into a desert' from Hugh Miller: 'Sutherland as it was and is' (1843)

'Now down on the shore the voice' from Adam Drinan: *The Ghosts of the Strath* (Fortune Press, 1943)

134 'Damn her, the old witch' quoted in John Prebble: *The Highland Clearances* (Secker and Warburg, 1963)

135 'A Shrath Nabhair 's a Shrath Chill Donnain/O Strathnaver' and 'Strath of Kildonan' from Derick Thomson: 'Srath Nabhair/Strathnaver' in *Creachadh na clarsaich/Plundering the Harp* (Macdonald, 1982)

'The thistles climb the thatch. Forever' – complete poem – Iain Crichton Smith: 'The Clearances' in *Selected Poems* (Carcanet, 1985)

'Ged thig anrach aineoil/Though a stranger, in his wanderings' from William Livingstone: 'Fios thun a' Bhaird/A Message to the Bard', translated Derick Thomson, in Roderick Watson ed. *The Poetry of Scotland* (Edinburgh University Press, 1995)

136 'The hearth-stone's black and cold/And sturdy grows the nettle' from Neil Munro: 'Nettles' in *The Poetry of Neil Munro* (Blackwood, 1931)

'very good grass-fields and corn-lands' from James Boswell: *The Journal of a Tour to the Hebrides* (Heinemann, 1936)

'Tha tim, an fiadh, an coille Hallaig/Time, the deer, is in the wood of Hallaig/Mura tig 's ann thearnas mi a Hallaig/I will go down to Hallaig' from Sorley MacLean: 'Hallaig' in *Complete Poems* by Sorley MacLean (Carcanet, 1993)

137 'At Burnmouth the door hangs from a broken hinge' from George Mackay Brown: 'Dead Fires' in *Selected Poems 1954–83* (John Murray, 1991) reproduced by permission of John Murray (Publishers) Ltd

'Oh it's awfully, frightfully nice/Picture it, if yous will/Take your oil-rigs by the score' from John McGrath: *The Cheviot, the Stag, and the Black, Black Oil* from *Six Pack: Plays for Scotland* (Polygon, 1996)

138 'Farewell to Lochaber, and farewell my Jean' from Allan Ramsay: 'Lochaber No More' in his *Poems* (1800)

'Bathgate no more' from The Proclaimers (Charlie and Craig Reid): 'Letter from America' [song] on *This is the Story* (1987). Words and Music by Charles Reid and Craig Reid, © 1987 Warner/Chappell Music Ltd, London W6 8BS, Lyrics reproduced by permission of IMP Ltd, all rights reserved

Chapter 16
page

141 'Now we ran among the birches' from R. L. Stevenson: *Kidnapped* (Penguin, 1994)

142 'Then clear the weeds from off his grave' from William Wordsworth: 'Rob Roy's Grave' in Dorothy Wordsworth: *Recollections of a Tour Made in Scotland* (Edinburgh: David Douglas, 1894)

'I wadna gie the finest sight we hae seen in the Highlands' from Walter Scott: *Rob Roy* (Originally published 1818. Modern edition Dent Everyman)

143 'barefooted, an old black kilt coat on' quoted from Eric Linklater: *The Prince in the Heather* (Hodder and Stoughton, 1965)

'He gave me no salutation' from R. L. Stevenson: *Kidnapped* (Penguin, 1994)

144 'The trunks of several trees had been wattled across' from R. L. Stevenson: *Kidnapped* (Penguin, 1994)

'The pass of Corryarick met us with a girning face/the sight of our tartan' from Neil Munro: *John Splendid* (B & W Publishing, 1994)

145 'There was no cover for a tomtit/I crawled out of my shelf' from John Buchan: *The Thirty-Nine Steps* (Penguin, 1956)

Chapter 17
page

147 'For Kilmeny had been she knew not where' from James Hogg: 'Kilmeny' in *Selected Poems and Songs* (Edinburgh: Scottish Academic Press, 1986)

'The muir is mirk, yet no wi' nicht' from Lewis Spence: 'Harmisay' in Rhoda Spence ed. *The Scottish Companion* (Edinburgh: Richard Paterson, 1955)

'There seemed to us to be nothing very particular about the island' from J. M. Barrie: *Mary Rose* in *Peter Pan and other plays* (Oxford World's Classics, 1995)

148 'These hymns were often heard at a great distance' from James Hogg: 'The Brownie of Bodsbeck' (Scottish Academic Press, 1976)

149   'As I was walking all alane' from 'The Twa Corbies' in William Beattie ed. *Border Ballads* (Penguin, 1952)
      'Peer more closely now' from Andrew Greig: *When They Lay Bare* (Faber and Faber, 1999)
      'Afore the brekk o day in the moarnin' from George Campbell Hay: 'Three Brothers' in *Collected Poems and Songs,* ed.
      Michel Byrne (Edinburgh University Press, 2000)
150   'They began to mock me' from Eric Linklater: 'Sealskin Trousers' in *The Goose Girl and Other Stories* (Canongate, 1991)
      'I am a man upon the land' from 'The Great Silkie of Sule Skerry' – traditional
151   'O I forbid you, maidens a'' from 'Tam Lin' in William Beattie ed. *Border Ballads* (Penguin, 1952)
152   'And if, as the story goes nine times out of ten' from Liz Lochhead: 'Tam Lin's Lady' in *Dreaming Frankenstein* (Polygon, 1984)
      'Sandy Nicoll saw him in the gloaming' from John Buchan: *Witch Wood* (Houghton Mifflin, 1927)
      'When, glimmering thro' the groaning trees' from Robert Burns: 'Tam o' Shanter' in *Poems and Songs* (Oxford University Press, 1969)
153   'Three horsemen rode between the hills' from George Mackay Brown: 'Witch' in *Selected Poems 1954–83* (John Murray, 1991)
      reproduced by permission of John Murray (Publishers) Ltd
      'It was my good-sister, it was Christian Shaw of Bargarran' from Naomi Mitchison: *The Bull Calves* (Jonathan Cape)
      'For the warlock's livin' yet' from Violet Jacob: 'The Rowan' in *The Scottish Poems of Violet Jacob* (Oliver and Boyd, 1944)
154   'It is his special night of freedom' from Duncan Williamson: *May the Devil walk behind ye!* (Canongate, 1989)
      'O thou, whatever title suit thee!' from Robert Burns: 'Address to the Deil' in *Poems and Songs* (Oxford University Press, 1969)
      'By looking at a person attentively' from James Hogg: *The Private Memoirs and Confessions of a Justified Sinner,* ed.
      Peter Garside (Edinburgh University Press, 2001)

Chapter 18

page

157   'Mars is braw in crammasy' from Hugh MacDiarmid: 'The Bonnie Broukit Bairn' in *Complete Poems* by Hugh MacDiarmid
      (Carcanet, 1993)
      'Skeins o geese write a word' from Kathleen Jamie: 'Skeins o geese' in *The Queen of Sheba* (Bloodaxe Books, 1994)
      'Sky is larger than life; land is small' from Robin Fulton: 'Clarities in Caithness'
      'The winter sun hangs just over the ridge of the Coolags' from George Mackay Brown: 'Maeshowe at Midwinter' in
      Under Brinkie's Brae (Gordon Wright, Edinburgh, 1979)
158   'If he worshipped the sun and the moon and the heavenly bodies' from F. Marian McNeill: *The Silver Bough*, vol. 1
      (William MacLellan, 1957)
      'Gloir dhuit fhein/Glory to thee/Failte dhut, a ghealach ur/Hail to thee, new moon' from *Carmina Gadelica,* vol. 3,
      ed. Alexander Carmichael (Oliver and Boyd, 1940)
159   'Glunta, owre aa' from Robert Alan Jamieson: 'Glunta (A fisherman's prayer)' in *Shoormal* (Polygon, 1986)
      'pay their daughters' tochers' from Neil Munro: *John Splendid* (B & W Publishing, 1994)
160   'Fog shroud' from Edwin Morgan: 'Guy Fawkes Moon' in *Collected Poems* by Edwin Morgan (Carcanet, 1993)
      'Saftly, saftly, throu the mirk' – complete poem – William Soutar: 'The Lanely Mune' in *Poems of William Soutar*
      (Scottish Academic Press, 1988)
161   'The Dog, and the Plough, and the Hunter, and all' from R. L. Stevenson: 'Escape at Bedtime' in *A Child's Garden of Verses*
      (originally published 1885)
      'Tae be wan o them Kings' – complete poem – George Mackay Brown 'Stars' from *Selected Poems 1954–83*
      (John Murray 1991) reproduced by permission of John Murray (Publishers) Ltd
      'Lionmhoireachd anns na speuran/Multitude of the skies' from Sorley MacLean: '*Lionmhoireachd*/Multitude' in *Complete Poems*
      by Sorley MacLean (Carcanet, 1993)
162   'I' the how-dumb-deid o' the cauld hairst nicht' from Hugh MacDiarmid: 'The Eemis Stane' in *Complete Poems* by
      Hugh MacDiarmid (Carcanet, 1993)
      'we went out in fireflauchts' from Edwin Morgan: 'Era' in *Collected Poems* (Carcanet, 1993)
      'It is black so. There is that dust' from Edwin Morgan: 'Thoughts of a Module' in *Collected Poems* (Carcanet, 1993)
163   'One is told about time blackout' from Naomi Mitchison: *Memoirs of a Spacewoman* (The Women's Press, 1985)
      'If ae rock conjures Scotland up for me' – complete poem – Colin Donati: 'Abuin them aa'

The Photographs and the Photographers

page

ii   Lairig Ghru towards Pools of Dee,
      Cairngorm Mountains *PB*
iv–v Line of forestry, Flow Country,
      Caithness *MA*
viii Ruined croft, Arnisdale, near
      Glenelg, Inverness-shire *PB*
3   Settlement remains, Truderscaig,
      Strathnaver, Sutherland *MA*
4   Coire Domhain, Cairngorm
      Mountains *PB*
5   Lochan nam bo Riabhach towards
      Morven, Caithness *PB*
7   (left & centre)
      Glencoe *MA*
7   (right)
      By Glencoe – Meall a Bhuiridh *MA*
10   A832 near Ullapool *MA*
11   Glencoe *MA*
12   Cloud formation *MA*
14   Glencoe *MA*
15   Blackless croft, Flow Country,
      Caithness *MA*
16   Deserted crofthouses, Gartymore,
      Sutherland *PB*
17   Broubster Village, Caithness *PB*
18, 19 (all)
      Dumfriesshire valley *MA*
20   Chambered Cairn, Cnoc na
      Maranaich, Dunbeath Strath,
      Caithness *PB*
21   Clach na h-Uaighhe and Cnoc a
      Chrochaidh, Kildonan, Sutherland *PB*
22   Inshriach Forest, Glen Feshie *PB*
23   Rothiemurchus *PB*
24   Inshriach Forest, Glen Feshie *PB*
25   Rothiemurchus *PB*
27   (left)
      Ferns on Branch *MA*
27   (right)
      Mossy rock with grass *MA*
28   Inshriach Forest, Glen Feshie *PB*
29   Rothiemurchus *PB*
30   Dunbeath Water, Caithness *PB*
31   Reflections *MA*
34   Waterfall, The Hermitage,
      Perthshire *MA*
35   Lochan, Caithness *MA*
37   Allt Creag an Leth-choin,
      Cairngorm Mountains *PB*

38   Thurso River and fisherman's bothy,
      Caithness *MA*
39   Loch Kishorn, towards Beinn Bhan *MA*
40   Stacks of Duncansby Head,
      Caithness *MA*
41   Tantallon Castle and the Bass Rock,
      East Lothian *MA*
42   Duart Point, Lismore Island *MA*
43   (left)
      Skye Bridge *MA*
43   (right)
      Isle of Stroma, Caithness *MA*
46   Thurso River and fisherman's bothy,
      Caithness *MA*
47   Rannoch Moor *MA*
50   Loch Rannoch *MA*
51   Lochan, Caithness *MA*
52   Storm, Eyemouth *MA*
54   (left)
      Fishing, Portmore Loch, Moorfoot
      Hills *MA*
54   (right)
      North Sea waves *MA*
55   Nets drying, Caithness *MA*
58   (left)
      Wick Harbour, fish market *MA*
58   (right)
      Fisherman's ropes, Wick *MA*
59   Lybster Harbour, Caithness *MA*
60   (left)
      Wick boatyard, winter maintenance of
      traditional fishing boat *MA*
60   (right)
      Wick boatyard, caulking traditional
      boat with oakum *MA*
61   Dunnet Head Lighthouse, looking
      towards Orkney *MA*
62, 63
      Cup and ring carvings, Ratho,
      near Edinburgh *MA*
64   Chambered Cairn, Cnoc na
      Maranaich, Dunbeath Strath,
      Caithness *PB*
65   Stone row, Torhousemuir,
      Galloway *PB*
66   Stow Church, Borders *MA*
67   Sinclair and Girnigoe Castle,
      Noss Head, near Wick *MA*

68   St Giles' Cathedral and the Old Town,
      Edinburgh: Scott Monument in
      foreground *MA*
69   (left)
      Gravestone, Abercorn Church *MA*
69   (right)
      Tombstones, skull and crossbones,
      by River Tay, Perthshire *MA*
70   Callanish, Lewis *MA*
71   Pilgrims' resting place en route to
      St Andrews *MA*
72   Rosslyn Chapel, Prentice Pillar *MA*
73   Merose Abbey, Melrose, Borders *MA*
74   Fields, Lammermuir Hills, by A68 *MA*
75   Moorland sheep pens, Borders *MA*
76, 77
      Fields, East Lothian *MA*
78   (left)
      Flagstone wall, Caithness *MA*
78   (right)
      Ruined croft, Duncansby,
      Caithness *MA*
79   (left)
      Abandoned farm machinery,
      Caithness *MA*
79   (right)
      Flagstone wall, Cliffs of Dunnet Head,
      Caithness *MA*
81   (left)
      Sheepfold, Truderscaig, Strathnaver,
      Caithness *PB*
81   (right)
      Achnacyth, Dunbeath Strath,
      Caithness *PB*
82   Marchmont House, Greenlaw,
      Borders *MP*
83   Smailholm Tower, near Kelso,
      Borders *MP*
86   Stornoway Castle, Lewis *MA*
87   Hume Castle, near Kelso, Borders *MP*
89   Broubster village, Caithness *PB*
90   Lochbuie Post Office, Mull *MA*
91   Wall with blue pipe, Portobello
      Promenade *MA*
92   Inter-village football match,
      Caithness *MA*
93   Salvation Army brass band,
      Wick Harbour *MA*

94 (left)
Window, deserted croft, Hoy *PB*

94 (right)
Ruined crofts, Caithness *MA*

95 Newton St Boswells noticeboard,
Borders *MA*

96 Inveraray, Loch Fyne *MA*

97 Borders Steam Railway *MA*

98 North Queensferry, Forth Rail Bridge
MA

99 Bo'ness steam railway, Falkirk *MA*

102 (left)
Wind farm, Lammermuir Hills,
Fala Moor *MA*

102 (right)
Mossmarain gas cracking plant, Fife
MA

103 (left & right)
Wind farm, Lammermuir Hills,
Fala Moor *MA*

104 Edinburgh, George Street:
King George, Assembly Halls and
The Hub in background *MA*

105 Edinburgh, Old Town Close,
looking towards Cockburn Street *MA*

108 (left)
Edinburgh Old Town in winter from
Princes Street *MA*

108 (right)
Glasgow skyline from Canal *MA*

111 (left)
Looking up Jackson's Close,
Old Town, Edinburgh *MA*

111 (right)
Leith from Calton Hill, Edinburgh *MA*

112 (left)
Charlotte Square, North side,
Edinburgh *MA*

112 (right)
Royal Circus, Circus Place,
Stockbridge and the New Town,
Edinburgh *MA*

114 Edinburgh, top of the Mound *MA*

115 Wester Hailes, Edinburgh *MA*

117 Natural basin in rock, Cairn Gorm *PB*

118 Cloud formations *MA*

119, 121
Callanish, Lewis *MA*

122 Melrose Abbey, Melrose, Borders *MA*

123 (left)
Iona, looking towards Mull, *MA*

123 (right)
Pilgrims' resting place en route to
St Andrews *MA*

124 The Eildon Hills from above Scott's
View *MA*

125 Coire an Lochain, Cairngorms *PB*

126 Flow Country, Caithness *MA*

127 Tree, Glenelg *PB*

128 Gypsy stall, Newton St Boswells,
Borders *MA*

129 Rothiemurchus *PB*

130 (left)
Bedford van, Caithness *MA*

130 (right)
Road across Kintyre, Arran mountains
in distance *MA*

131 Old Drove Road, near Broughton,
Borders *MA*

132 Broubster village, Caithness *PB*

133 Crofthouse interior, Crofts of
Benachielt, Latheron, Caithness *PB*

134 Gravestone and railings, Kirkmaiden,
Monreith, Galloway *PB*

135 (left)
The Great Slab, Cairn Lochan,
Cairngorm Mountains *PB*

135 (right)
Afforrested site of Ceann-na coille,
Strathnaver, Sutherland *PB*

136 (left)
Grumbeg, Strathnaver, Sutherland *PB*

136 (centre)
Cloud formation *MA*

136 (right)
Coire Domhain, Cairngorm
Mountains *PB*

137 (left)
Long house remains, Dailmallart,
Strathnaver, Caithness *PB*

137 (right)
Dyke, Learable Township, Strath
Uillie, Sutherland *PB*

139 Ruined croft, Arnisdale, near Glenelg,
Inverness-shire *PB*

140 Flow Country, Caithness *MA*

141 Broch, Dunbeath Caithness *PB*

142 (left)
Borders sheep pens *MA*

142 (centre)
Moorland peat cut vertically,
Caithness *MA*

142 (right)
Early afforestation programme
Sutherland *MA*

143 Satellite photograph of Ben Alder *Sat*

144 (left)
Dunbeath Water towards Wag Hill,
Dunbeath Strath, Caithness *PB*

144 (centre & right)
Cairngorm Mountains *PB*

145 Creag naFhithich, Dunbeath Strath,
Caithness *PB*

146 Above Broughton, Borders *MA*

147 Angel in Winter, Roslin Graveyard *MA*

148 Site of Wester Badanloch,
Loch Badanloch, Caithness *PB*

148 Cairn, Rosal, Strathnaver,
Sutherland *PB*

149 (left)
Graveyard, Isle of Harris *MA*

149 (centre)
Spider's web, Inshriach Forest,
Glen Feshie *PB*

149 (right)
Angel, Marchmont Cemetery,
Edinburgh *MA*

150 (left)
Near Erbusaig, Kyle of Lochalsh *MA*

150 (right)
Loch Lomond from Ben Lomond *MA*

151 (left)
Near Howgate, Midlothian *MA*

151 (right)
The Cobbler, Highlands *MA*

152 Cairngorm Mountains *PB*

153 Ruins, Dunbeath Strath, Caithness *PB*

154 The Highlands *MA*

155 Sunburst, Skye *PB*

156 Natural basin in rock, Cairn Gorm *PB*

157 Cobwebs and dew, Birse, Deeside *PB*

158 Chapel Hill, Balachly, Dunbeath,
Caithness *PB*

159 Looking south over Caithness to
Morven *MA*

159 Callanish, Lewis *MA*

160 Sun breaking through clouds *MA*

161 St Ninian's Cave, Port Castle Bay,
Galloway *PB*

162 (left)
Lichen pattern, Corwall Port,
Galloway *PB*

162 (centre)
Caithness flagstone *MA*

162 (right)
Satellite image of Crowlin Island,
West Coast *Sat*

163 Stone circle, Torhousemuir,
Galloway *PB*

164 Angel, Marchmont Cemetery,
Edinburgh *MA*

PB   Paul Basu
MA   Marius Alexander
MP   Morris Paton
Sat   Landsat

Index of Places

Abbotsford, 84
   Bemersyde (Scott's View), 1
   Cauldshiels Loch, 32
Aberdeen, 105, 106, 107–8
Aberdeenshire, 76
   Mither Tap, 10
Aberfoyle, 142
Abernethy Forest, 25
Aikey, 78
Aikwood Tower, Ettrickdale, 123
Altrive lake, 79
'An Cuilithionn/The Cuillin, 10–11
Angus
   Glen Ogil, 19, 20
   Glen Prosen, 19, 20
   Glenesk, 19, 20
Annaty Burn, near Scone, 65
Anstruther, 57
Aonach Beag, 6
Appin, 143
Arbuthnott, 68
Argyll, 129
   Etive River, 33
   Glen Aora, 136
   Glencoe, 17, 18, 19, 21, 119, 147,
     149
   Inveraray, 85, 86, 92, 145
   Lochfyneside, 127
   Moor of Rannoch, 5
Arran, 41, 42
Assynt, 1, 11
Ayrshire, 75, 79, 102

Baile-chuirn, 27
Bailie an Òr, 17
Balquhidder, 141–2, 144
Banff, 91
Barra, 158
Barra Head, 48
Bedlay, 85
Beinn a'Ghlo, 152
Beinn Bhreac, 8
Beinn Bhrotain, Cairngorms, 119
Beinn Dearg, 8
Beinn Dòbhrain/Ben Dorain, 11
Bemersyde (Scott's View), 1
Ben Alder (Loch Ericht), Cluny's Cage, 143,
   144
Ben Bulben, County Sligo, 119

Ben Dorain/Beinn Dòbhrain, 149
Ben Nevis, 6, 10, 50
Bennachie, 10
Bharrain, 41
Black Cart River, Renfrewshire, 99
Black Isle, 125
Black Wood of Rannoch, 26
Blair Atholl, Falls of Bruar, 37
Bonnington Linn, Falls of Clyde, 37
Braeriach, 8
Braes of Gleniffer, 9
Braes of Glenmoriston, 143
Brodgar, Orkney, 65
Broughton, Tweeddale, 28
Buachaille Etive Beag, Argyll, 17
Buachaille Etive Mor, Argyll, 17
Buchan, 75, 77, 78
Bute, 41
Butt of Lewis, 48

Caenlochan forest, 19
Cairngorms, 8, 13, 31
   Beinn Bhrotain, 119
   Coire Cath nam Fionn, 119
   Glen Derry, 26
Caithness, 56, 157
   Dunbeath Strath, 66
   Dunbeath Water, 34
Caledon, Great Wood of, 23–8
Caledonian Canal (hill of Tomnahurich),
   124
Callanish, Lewis, 65, 157
Candida Casa, Whithorn, 121
Canongate kirkyard, Edinburgh, 110
Carn an Tuirc, 119
Càrn Cùl ri Eirinn, Iona, 122
Carradale, 58, 87, 95
Cauldshiels Loch, Abbotsford, 32
Cluny's Cage, Ben Alder (Loch Ericht), 143,
   144
Clyde, River, 36–7, 100, 103, 121
Clydesdale, 76
   Clydes Burn, 36
   Daer Water, 36
   Potrail Burn, 36
Cnoc na Aingeal ('hill of the angels')
   (Sìthean Mòr ['big fairy hill']), Iona,
   122
Coille Naise, 21

Coire Cath nam Fionn, Cairngorms, 119
Corra Linn, Falls of Clyde, 37
Corrieyairack, 8
County Sligo, Ben Bulben, 119
Craigannet, Stirlingshire, 65
Craigrostan, Loch Lomond, 141
Crieff, Sma' Glen, 119
Croick parish church, Easter Ross, 134
Cromarty, 65
Cubbie Roo's Castle, Wyre, 45
Culbin Sands, Moray Firth, 53
Culloden, 124, 142

Daer Water, Clydesdale, 36
Dee River, 33
Deeside, 106
Doune of Rothiemurchus, 84
Druim a' Ghiùbhsaich, Loch Arkaig, 26
Drummossie Moor, 124
Dryburgh, 66
Dubh Artach (off Mull), 60
Dumfriesshire, 79
   Ewes River, 35
   Langholm, 35, 92, 162
   Wauchope River, 35
Dunadd, 123
Dunaverty, Kintyre, 123
Dunbeath Strath, Caithness, 66
Dunbeath Water, Caithness, 34
Dundee, 53, 101, 105, 108–9
Duneaves, Perthshire, 65
Dunndaff, Falls of Clyde, 37
Dunskaith, Skye, 43

Earlston (Ercildoune), 123
Eas na Smuid (Falls of Foyers), Loch Ness, 38
East Anglia, 56
East Lothian, 75
Easter Ross, Croick parish church, 134
Edinburgh, 11, 12, 95–6, 99, 103, 105,
   109–12, 160
   Canongate kirkyard, 110
   Goose Pie House, 110
   Greyfriars' Kirkyard, 12
   Mary King's Close, 112
   Parliament Square, 112
   Royal Mile, 70, 110
   St Cuthbert's, 66
   Tron Kirk bell, 69–70

Eildon Hills, 1, 123
Eildon Tree, 124
Eilean a'Cheò, Skye, 42
Eilean Dearg, Loch Katrine, 141
Eilean nam Ban ('isle of the women'), 122
Eillisland, 79
Ercildoune (Earlston), 123
Ericht River, Perthshire, 99
Erraid, 60
Etive River, Argyll, 33
Ettrick Forest, 28
Ettrickdale, Aikwood Tower, 123
Ewes River, Dumfriesshire, 35

Falls of Bruar, Blair Atholl, 37
Falls of Clyde, 38
        Bonnington Linn, 37
        Corra Linn, 37
        Dundaff, 37
        Stonebyres, 37
Falls of Foyers (Eas na Smuid),
        Loch Ness, 38
Falls of Measach, Wester Ross, 38
Fèinne-bheinn, Loch Hope (Sutherland),
        119
Fingal's Cave, Staffa, 119
Fionn's Seat (Suidhe Fhinn), Portree, 119
Firth of Clyde, 41
        Bute, 41
Firth of Tay, 53
Flannan Isles, west of Lewis, 61
Forfar, Angus, 19, 20
Forres, 106
Fort Augustus, 24
Forth Bridge, 102–3
Forth and Clyde Canal, 100, 102
Fortingall, Perthshire, 26
Foula, 47
Fraserburgh, 57
Fife, St Andrews, 24

Galloway, 145
Gallowsha, Kirkwall, 153
Garbh Bheinn, 6
Gask, 83
Glasgow, 36, 41, 100, 102, 103, 105, 108,
        112–15, 115, 121
        Glasgow Cathedral, 67
        Glasgow Green, 99, 113
        Gorbals, 114
        Kelvingrove, 113
Glen Affric, 25
Glen Aora, Argyll, 136
Glen Clova, 20
        Angus, 19, 20
Glen Derry, Cairngorms, 26
Glen Etive, 21
        house of Dalness, 145
Glen Ogil, Angus, 19, 20
Glen Orchy, Argyll, 12
Glen Prosen, Angus, 19, 20
Glencoe, Argyll, 17, 18, 19, 21, 119, 147,
        149
Glenesk, Angus, 19, 20
Glengyle, Loch Katrine, 141
Glens of Angus, 19, 20
Golspie, 135
Goose Pie House, Edinburgh, 110
Gorbals, Glasgow, 114
Great Glen, 142
Greenock, Renfrewshire, 100
Grey Mare's Tail, Moffat, 38

Greyfriars' Kirkyard, Edinburgh, 12
Grieve House, Whalsay, 47

Haddington, East Lothian, 91–2
Hallaig, Raasay, Skye, 136
Hamnavoe (Stromness), 46, 91
Helmsdale, 16
Hirta (St Kilda), 50
Holy Isle, 42
Houston, Renfrewshire, 85
Hoy (Orkney), Trowie Glen, 151
Hoy Sound, Orkney, 161

Inveraray, Argyll, 85, 86, 92, 145
Inverlochy, 18, 144, 145
Inverness, 105
Inversnaid, Stob an Fhainne, 119
Iona, 65, 121–3, 147
        Càrn Cùl ri Eirinn, 122
        Cnoc na Aingeal ('hill of the angels')
            (Sìthean Mòr ['big fairy hill']), 122
        Port a' Churaich, 122
        Tòrr an Aba ('hill of the abbot'), 122
Islay, 135

Jedburgh, 66

Kelso, 66
Kelvingrove, Glasgow, 113
Kildonan burn, 17
Kingsburgh House, Skye, 44
Kingussie, 25
Kinraddie, Lewis, 68
Kintyre, 42, 129
        Carradale, 87
        Dunaverty, 123
Kirk Allowat, 154
Kirk Yetholm, 128
Kirkintilloch, 85
Kirkwall Cathedral, 68
Kirriemuir, Angus, 19, 20, 93

Lake District, 10
Lamlash, 42
Lanarkshire, Leadhills, 99
Langholm, Dumfriesshire, 35, 92, 162
Langloan (now part of Coatbridge,
        Lanarkshire), 100
Leadhills, Lanarkshire, 99
Levern River, Renfrewshire, 99
Lewis, 41, 48, 120
        Kinraddie, 68
Linwood, 101
Liverpool, 108
Loch Arkaig, Druim a'Ghiùbhsaich, 26
Loch Awe, 32
Loch Ericht, Ben Alder, Cluny's Cage, 143,
        144
Loch Etive, 20
Loch Fyne, 57, 58
Loch Hope (Sutherland), Fèinne-bheinn,
        119
Loch Katrine
        Eilean Dearg, 141
        Glengyle, 141
Loch Lomond, 15, 31
        Craigrostan, 141
        Inversnaid, Stob an Fhainne, 119
Loch Morar (Morag), 32
Loch Ness, 32
        Falls of Foyers (Eas na Smuid), 38
Loch Triochatan, 17

Loch Voshimid, Harris, 147
Lochfyneside, Argyll, 127

Maeshowe, Brodgar, Orkney, 157
Mallaig, 57
Mary King's Close, Edinburgh, 112
Melrose, 66
Melrose Abbey, 123
Minch (Struth nam Fera Gorma), 56, 150
Mither Tap, Aberdeenshire, 10
Moffat, Grey Mare's Tail, 38
Moor of Rannoch, Argyll, 5
Morar, 50
Moray Firth, Culbin Sands, 53
Mount Benger, 79
Muckle Flugga, Shetland, 60
Muir of Ord, 124
Mull, 44

Oban, 25, 95
Ord of Caithness, 16
Orkney, 32, 41, 45, 46, 105, 150, 153
        Brodgar, 157
        Kirkwall Cathedral, 68
        Orphir, 45
        Skara Brae, 53
Outer Hebrides, 150

Paisley, 9, 153
Papa Stour, 47
Parliament Square, Edinburgh, 112
Peebles, 91
Pentland Hills, 8
Perth, 105, 108
Perthshire, 129
        Duneaves, 65
        Ericht River, 99
        Fortingall, 26
        Schiehallion, 13
Peterhead, 57
Pittenweem, 57
Port a' Churaich, Iona, 122
Portree (Skye), Suidhe Fhinn (Fionn's Seat),
        119
Potrail Burn, Clydesdale, 36
Powsail Burn, Tweeddale, 28
Princes Street, Edinburgh, 110

Raasay (Skye), Hallaig, 136
Ramsay Garden, Edinburgh, 110
Rannoch Moor, 144
Renfrewshire
        Black Cart River, 99
        Greenock, 100
        Houston, 85
        Levern River, 99
Ring of Brodgar, Orkney, 157
Rosneath, Dunbartonshire, 65
Rosslyn Chapel, 72
Rowardennan, 141
Royal Mile, Edinburgh, 70, 110

St Andrews, 24
St Cuthbert's, Edinburgh, 66
St Kilda (Hirta), 50
St Ninian's, Whithorn, 66
St Ninian's Isle, Shetland, 121
Scalloway Castle, Shetland, 85
Schiehallion, Perthshire, 13
Sgriob na Cailleach, Paps of Jura, 152
Sgurr Alasdair, Cuillin, Skye, 10
Shepherds of Etive, Argyll, 17

Shetland, 41, 45, 56, 87, 107–8, 150
    Muckle Flugga, 60
    St Ninian's Isle, 121
    Scalloway Castle, 85
    Sullom Voe, 48
Sìthean Mòr ('big fairy hill') (Cnoc na
    aingeal ['hill of the angels']), Iona,
    122
Skara Brae, Orkney, 53
Skerryvore (south west of Tiree), 60
Skye, 15, 41, 45, 120, 142
    Cuillin, Sgurr Alasdair, 10
    Eilean a'Cheo, 42
    Kingsburgh House, 44
    Portree, Suidhe Fhinn (Fionn's Seat),
    119
    Raasay, Hallaig, 136
Sma' Glen, Crieff, 119
South Uist, 120, 142
Spean Bridge, 26
Spey River, 35–6
Staffa, Fingal's Cave, 119
Stirlingshire, Craigannet, 65

Stob an Fhainne, Inversnaid (Loch Lomond),
    119
Stob Choire Claurigh, 6
Stob Grianan, 21
Stonebyres, Falls of Clyde, 37
Strath of Kildonan, Sutherland, 16, 17, 133
Strath Naver, Sutherland, 16, 133
Strathspey, 25
Strathyre, 15
Stromness (Hamnavoe), 46, 91
Struth nam Fera Gorma (Minch), 150
Suidhe Fhinn (Fionn's Seat), Portree, 119
Suisgill burns, 17
Sullom Voe, Shetland, 48
Summerlee, 100
Sutherland, 129
    Loch Hope, Fèinne-bheinn, 119
    Strath of Kildonan, 133
    Strath Naver, 133

Tarbert, 57
Tay Bridge, 109
Tay River, 99

Taynuilt, 21
Tomnahurich (near Inverness), 26
Tòrr an Aba ('hill of the abbot'), Iona, 122
Torran Rocks (off Mull), 60
Tron Kirk bell, Edinburgh, 69–70
Trossachs, 141, 142
Trowie Glen, Hoy (Orkney), 151
Tweed River, 1, 123
Tweeddale, 120
    Broughton, 28
    Powsail Burn, 28
Tyndrum, 25

Wanlockhead (near Leadhills), 99
Wauchope River (Dumfriesshire), 35
Wester Ross, 129
Western Isles, 142
Whalsay, 47
Whithorn, Candida Casa, 121
Wyre, 45
    Cubbie Roo's Castle, 45

Yarrow, 147

Index of Names

Aboulela, Leila, 108
Alasdair, Alasdair MacMhaighstir, 53–4
Argyll, Duke of, 86
Arthur (King of Britain), 28

Bàn, Donnchadh, 12
Banks, Iain M., 163
Barrie, Sir J. M., 20, 28, 93, 147
Bateman, Meg, 15
Bjarni (son of Kolbein Hruga), 45
Blake, George, 103
Bonnie Prince Charlie (Prince Charles
    Edward Stuart, 31, 43, 83, 142–3
Boswell, James, 24, 44, 136
Brahan Seer (Coinneach Odhar Fiosaiche;
    Kenneth the Knowledgeable), 124–5
Breadalbane, Lord, 12
Bride, St (St Brigid), 120
Brooksbank, Mary, 101
Brown, George Douglas, 94
Brown, George Mackay, 46, 65, 68, 91,
    111, 127, 130, 137, 153, 157–8, 161
Buchan, John (1st Baron Tweedsmuir),
    23, 28, 36, 145, 152
Burgess, J. J. Haldane, 87
Burns, Robert, 9, 37–8, 69, 70, 71, 75,
    75–6, 79, 85–6, 110, 154
Burnside, John, 109
Byron, Lord (George Gordon), 106

Cailte (Fionn's nephew), 120
Campbell of Glenlyon, Captain Robert, 18
Campbell, Thomas, 100
Carlyle, Jane (née Welsh), 91–2, 96
Carlyle, Thomas, 91
Carswell, John (bp of the Isles), 120
Clarinda (friend of Robert Burns), 110
Cockburn, Lord, 91, 105
Coinneach Odhar Fiosaiche (the Brahan
    Seer; Kenneth the Knowledgeable),
    124–5

Coleridge, Samuel Taylor, 10, 37
Columba, St, 32, 33, 65, 121–3, 147
Columbus, Christopher, 72
Conchobar (Irish king), 21
Corrie, Joe, 101
Crichton Smith, Iain, 11, 41, 48, 53, 56,
    106–7, 111, 134, 135
Cruickshank, Helen B., 1, 13, 19, 34–5, 55,
    68–9

Davidson, John, 100
Defoe, Daniel, 141
Deirdre, 21
Donati, Colin, 102–3, 163
Drinan, Adam, 133–4
Dunbar, William, 106
Dunn, Douglas, 50
Dutton, G. F., 5–6

Ettrick Shepherd (James Hogg), 10, 27, 28,
    79, 123, 147, 148, 151, 154

Faed, Thomas, 134
Fair Duncan of the Songs (Donnchadh Bàn
    Mac an t-Saoir [Duncan Ban
    Macintyre]), 11–12, 65
Fencibles, Crochallan, 76
Fergusson, Robert, 69–70, 110, 112
Fianna, 120, 125
Fingal, 119
Finlay, Ian Hamilton, 58–9
Fionn, 120
Fionn mac Cumhaill (Finn MacCool), 119
Fraser, G. S., 107
Fraser, Olive, 5
Fulton, Robin, 42, 157

Galt, John, 41, 67, 92, 99, 127–8
Garioch, Robert, 110–12
Garry, Flora, 10, 75, 79–80
Geddes, James Young, 108

Gibbon, Lewis Grassic, 65, 68–9, 80, 81,
    105
Gibson, Wilfrid Wilson, 61
Glencairn, Earl of, 85–6
Gordon, George (Lord Byron), 106
Gordon, Madge (queen of the Yetholm
    gipsies), 128
Gorman, Rody, 6–7, 35–6
Grant, Elizabeth of Rothiemurchus, 24–5,
    84
Gray, Alasdair, 67, 115
Gray, Alexander, 75
Greig, Andrew, 149
Gunn, Neil, 2, 9, 16, 20–1, 34, 50, 55, 66,
    133

Hamilton, Ian, 113–14
Hamilton, Janet, 99, 100–1
Hay, George Campbell, 53, 54, 57–8,
    149–50
Hay, John MacDougall, 57
Hays of Errol, 27
Henderson, Hamish, 130
Herbert, W. N., 109
Hind, Archie, 115
Hogg, James (the Ettrick Shepherd), 10, 27,
    28, 79, 123, 147, 148, 151, 154
Hopkins, Gerard Manley, 31
Hruga, Kolbein, 45

Irving, Washington, 151

Jacob, Violet, 72, 93, 130
James V, King of Scotland, 28
Jamie, Kathleen, 157
Jamieson, Robert Alan, 47, 48, 85, 159
Jenkins, Win, 105
Johnson, Dr Samuel, 24, 44, 91, 120, 136
Johnston, Ellen, 101
Johnston, Paul, 163

Keats, John, 10, 75
Kelman, James, 115
Kennedy, A. L., 15
Kenneth the Knowledgeable (Coinneach Odhar Fiosaiche; the Brahan Seer), 124–5
Kentigern, St (St Mungo), 120, 121
Kesson, Jessie, 80, 107
Kieran, St, 65
Kincaid, John, 113
Kirk, Revd Robert (minister of Aberfoyle), 152

Laidlaw of Phaup, Will, 147–8
Leonard, Tom, 101, 115
Lermontov, Mikhail Yuriyevich, 123
Linklater, Eric, 45, 150
Livingstone, William (Uilleam MacDhùnlèibhe), 135–6
Lochhead, Liz, 31, 115, 151–2
Lyndsay, Sir David, 121

Mac an t-Saoir, Donnchadh Bàn (Duncan Ban Macintyre; 'Fair Duncan of the Songs'), 11–12, 65
McArthur, Alexander, 114
MacCaig, Norman, 1, 11, 13, 38, 111
MacColla, Fionn, 134
MacCool, Finn (Fionn mac Cumhaill), 119
McCrone, Guy, 113
MacDhùnlèibhe, Uilleam (William Livingstone), 135–6
MacDiarmid, Hugh, 1, 10, 17, 21, 35, 47, 71, 75, 92, 105, 111, 157, 162
MacDonald, Flora, 43, 142
Macfarlan, James, 100
MacGill, Patrick, 101
McGonagall, William, 108–9, 113
McGrath, John, 137–8
MacGregor, Rob Roy, 128, 141–2
McIlvanney, William, 102
Macintosh, Denis, 58
Macintyre, Duncan Ban (Donnchadh Bàn Mac an t-Saoir; 'Fair Duncan of the Songs'), 11–12, 65
Mackenzie, Sir Compton, 48
Maclain (chief of the MacDonalds of Glencoe), 18
Maclaren, Ian, 93
McLean, Duncan, 78–9
MacLean, Sorley (Somerled MacGill-Eain), 10–11, 26–7, 43, 111, 136–7, 161–2
McLellan, Robert, 36, 42, 76
MacLeod, Ken, 163
MacNeacail, Aonghas, 15
McNeill, F. Marian, 158
Macpherson, Cluny, 143, 144
Macpherson, James, 119
Macpherson, John, 120
Macpherson, Mary (Màiri Mhòr nan Oran; 'Big Mary of the Songs'), 15
Magnus, St, 68
Martin, Angus, 41
Merlin, 28, 120
Miller, Hugh, 133
Mitchison, Naomi, 17, 42, 58, 83, 86, 87, 95, 131, 153, 163
Moffat, Alexander, 111
Montrose, Duke of, 141

Moon, Lorna, 94–5
Mor, MacCailein (Marquis of Argyll), 145
Morgan, Edwin, 23, 103, 111, 114, 115, 121–2, 123, 159–60, 162
Muir, Edwin, 45, 46, 91, 105
Muir, William, 100
Mungo, St (St Kentigern), 120, 121
Munro, Neil, 5, 18–19, 56, 92, 136, 144, 145, 159
Murray, Charles, 76, 77, 79

Nairne, Lady Carolina (née Oliphant), 83
Naoise, 21
Neill, William, 119
Ninian, St, 121

Oig, Robin (Rob Roy MacGregor's son), 144
Oliphant, Carolina (by marriage Lady Nairne), 83
Oliphant, Charles, 83
Oliphant, Charlotte, 83
Oran, Màiri Mhòr nan (Mary Macpherson; 'Big Mary of the Songs'), 15
O'Rourke, Donny, 115
Osborne, Lloyd, 25
Ossian, 17, 119, 120

Paterson, Don, 109
Patrick, St, 120
Pilate, Pontius, 26
Prebble, John, 16

Rafferty, Sean, 127
Raghnaill, Birlinn Chlann, 53
Ramsay, Allan, 99, 110, 138
Rankin, Ian, 72, 107–8, 112
Rendall, Robert, 46
Robert the Bruce (King of Scotland), 123
Robertson, Jeannie, 130
Robertson, Stanley, 130
Robertson, T. A., 47

Scot, Michael, 123, 125
Scott, Alexander, 106
Scott, Andrew Murray, 53
Scott, Sir Peter, 32
Scott, Sir Walter, 1, 28, 32, 38, 41, 59, 66, 67, 72, 79, 84, 109, 123, 128, 141, 142
Scott, Tom, 70–1
Seaforth, Countess of, 125
Seaforth, Earl of, 125
Sellar, Patrick, 134
Shakespeare, William, 106
Shaw, Christian, 153
Shepherd, Nan, 8, 13, 33, 50
Smith, Alexander, 9, 36–8, 112–13
Smith, Sydney Goodsir, 38–9, 111
Smollett, Tobias, 105
Somerled MacGill-Eain (Sorley MacLean), 136–7
Soutar, William, 8–9, 87–8, 160
Southey, Robert, 59, 67
Spark, Muriel, 111
Spence, Lewis, 70, 147
Stevenson, Robert (engineer), 60
Stevenson, Robert Louis, 8, 9, 19, 25, 44, 59, 60–1, 105, 110, 111, 141, 143–4, 145, 160–1
Stewart, Earl Patrick, 85
Stowe, Harriet Beecher, 67

Stuart, Prince Charles Edward (Bonnie Prince Charlie), 31, 43, 83, 142–3
Sutherland, Duke of, 135

Tannahill, Robert, 9
Thomas the Rhymer, 27, 123–4, 125, 151
Thomson, Derick, 48–9, 51–7, 106, 134–5, 556–7
Torrington, Jeff, 101, 114
Toulmin, David, 78
Trocchi, Alexander, 102

'Vagaland', 54–5
Veitch, John, 147
Victoria (Queen of Great Britain), 17, 18, 21

Walterson, F. S., 48
Warner, Alan, 95–6
Watson, Walter, 85
Watt, James, 99
Welsh, Irvine, 112
Welsh, Jane (wife of Thomas Carlyle), 91–2, 96
Whyte, Betsy, 129
William III (King of Britain), 18
Williamson, Duncan, 127, 130, 131, 154
Wilson, John, 37
Wordsworth, Dorothy, 37
Wordsworth, William, 10, 37, 119, 141–2

Yeats, W. B., 119
Young, Andrew, 53